WALKING
with
JESUS

WALKING
with
JESUS

Devotions for Advent & Christmas 2024

Editors of *Mornings with Jesus*

A GUIDEPOSTS DEVOTIONAL

A Gift from Guideposts

Thank you for your purchase! We want to express our gratitude for your support with a special gift just for you.

Dive into *Spirit Lifters*, a complimentary e-book that will fortify your faith, offering solace during challenging moments. Its 31 carefully selected scripture verses will soothe and uplift your soul.

Please use the QR code or go to **guideposts.org/ spiritlifters** to download.

Walking with Jesus: Devotions for Advent & Christmas 2024

Published by Guideposts
100 Reserve Road, Suite E200
Danbury, CT 06810
Guideposts.org

Cover and interior design by Pamela Walker, W Design Studio
Cover photo by Dreamstime
Typeset by Aptara, Inc.

ISBN 978-1-961441-16-3 (softcover)
ISBN 978-1-961441-17-0 (epub)

Printed and bound in the United States of America

A Christmas Blessing for You
May Jesus, our Savior,
Who was born on Christmas Day,
Bless you at this season
In a very special way.
May the beauty and the promise
Of that silent, holy night
Fill your heart with peace and happiness
And make your new year bright!

Helen Steiner Rice

INTRODUCTION

Advent is a time of joyful anticipation. We look forward to the festivities of Christmas and the bustle of shopping, planning, and decorating that come before. Advent is also a time of prayerful preparation as we near an event of great significance to our spiritual identity. *Walking with Jesus: Devotions for Advent & Christmas 2024* helps ready us to celebrate Jesus's birth and the prospect of His return. The devotions lead us in hopeful, grateful steps away from the hubbub, distractions, and troubles of daily life and toward a closer relationship with our Redeemer, whose love for us is constant.

The word *Advent*, which means "coming" or "arrival" in Latin, never appears in the Bible, though the hallmarks of Advent are documented in scripture. The first Nativity had been foretold for generations. Indeed, preparations and prophecies for the earthly arrival of the Savior had been ongoing since the days of the Old Testament. The words of the prophet Isaiah, immortalized in George Frideric Handel's masterpiece *Messiah,* are a grand example.

> For unto us a child is born, unto us a son
> is given: and the government shall be
> upon his shoulder: and his name shall be
> called Wonderful, Counsellor, The mighty God,
> The everlasting Father, The Prince of Peace.
> Isaiah 9:6 (KJV)

Isaiah had a lot to say about the coming of the Lord, long before His humble manger birth. And people were listening to and repeating the same prophecies (even if many were failing to recognize the fulfillment of the scriptures as Jesus walked among them). Note how John references the prophet years after the Lord's Resurrection:

> Isaiah said this because he saw Jesus' glory and spoke about him.
> John 12:41 (NIV)

Our 2024 Advent calendar begins on Sunday, December 1, when we enter a time for reflecting on the birth and significance of Christ in our world and preparing ourselves for His second coming. To help in that aim, a group of talented devotional writers share their insights and spiritual encouragement in this devotional. You'll find that every day of Advent is anchored and clarified by three devotions—each a personal story with spiritual resonance, coupled with a scripture quote. Each devotion also includes a faith step—a question or suggestion to help direct your spiritual path. The devotions mirror the weekly themes of Advent: Hope, Peace, Joy, and Love:

Hope can lighten our load and build our courage in a world that may seem unkind, hostile, even dangerous. Remember Zechariah's words to his newborn son, John the Baptist:

"And you, my child, will be called a prophet of the Most High;
for you will go on before the Lord to prepare the way for him,
to give his people the knowledge of salvation
through the forgiveness of their sins."
Luke 1:76–77 (NIV)

Having faith that Christ will save us and forgive our sins makes living a hopeful act: Reward and redemption can always come through the grace of God.

Peace settles our minds and calms our spirits amid demanding routines that would otherwise drain us and perils that could threaten to overwhelm. Once again, Zechariah's prophecy touches on the healing tranquility that can be ours through Jesus:

"The rising sun will come to us from heaven
to shine on those living in darkness
and in the shadow of death, to guide our feet
into the path of peace."
Luke 1:78–79 (NIV)

Joy enables us to treasure the life we have today and sustains us into the future. Imagine how the shepherds felt in the wake of the angels' announcement of the holy birth—so amazed and changed by news of Christ's arrival that they had to see Him for themselves. After visiting the stable, they could not contain their rapture:

> The shepherds returned, glorifying and praising
> God for all the things they had heard and seen,
> which were just as they had been told.
> Luke 2:20 (NIV)

Love brings us closest to the realm of God, our maker and sustainer, who cherishes us despite our imperfections. We are told to love each other, just as Jesus taught His disciples on earth:

> "My command is this: Love each other as I have loved you."
> John 15:12 (NIV)

By inviting the themes of Advent into your heart, you can embrace them in your soul. You may opt to read our three daily devotions at morning, noon, and evening—reflecting on how each speaks to you at that moment—or you might find it more fulfilling to read them all at once, immersing yourself in the writers' faithful counsel and seeking the direction of the Holy Spirit. Consider sharing these devotions with loved ones, opening yourself to others' interpretations. Even if you're not in the habit of reading devotions, you'll find that Advent is a resonant time to begin.

You might use the dedicated space at the end of this book to record the season's special moments—the impressions and memories that brightened this Advent and Christmas. Or you might write down your reflections and progress on specific devotions and faith steps, forming a sort of spiritual time capsule. You and your family can look back and marvel at this journey of faith.

The days leading up to Christ's birth may be fleeting, but the deep lessons they impart can enrich us and usher us ever closer to God's grace. May your season be full of hope, peace, joy, and love!

Lisa Guernsey

HOPE

God of Hope, thank You for giving us
new birth into a living hope through
the Resurrection of Jesus Christ. Thank
you for giving us an inheritance that
can never perish, spoil, or fade.

Our hope does not put us to shame,
because Your love has been poured out into
our hearts. Remind us that the Scriptures
were written to teach us and that the
encouragement they provide gives us hope.
Grant that we may overflow with hope by
the power of the Holy Spirit. Amen.

First Sunday of Advent, December 1

You will be secure, because there is hope; you will look about you and take your rest in safety. Job 11:18 *(NIV)*

My husband and I were new members of our Lutheran church. We were still getting to know the others in the congregation, so when the pastor asked us to light the first violet candle on the Advent wreath, I hesitated. But my husband smiled broadly and spoke up. "We'd be honored!"

Immediately, I began thinking of everything that could go wrong. *What if I stumbled? What if I have trouble getting the candle lit?*

I knew so little about the Advent wreath. All I could remember was the first candle stood for hope and the word *Advent* meant *coming.* "Well, hope is the right candle for me," I told Jesus. I hoped I'd do okay.

When we got home, I did what everyone does: I started combing through the internet. It cleared up all of my questions, and I understood more about Advent. But the phrases that captured my attention the most were "holy anticipation fulfilled by the life and death of Christ" and "the hope we have in Christ." I prayerfully pondered these words all week.

That first Sunday of Advent, when it was time for my husband and me to go to the front of the church and light the candle, I did so with hope in Jesus, not in myself. —Jeannie Hughes

---

Faith Step: *Think of a way you have lost hope in yourself. Pray about it and ask Jesus how you can instead put that hope in Him.*

First Sunday of Advent, December 1

For in this hope we were saved. But hope that is seen is no hope at all. Who hopes for what they already have? But if we hope for what we do not yet have, we wait for it patiently. Romans 8:24–25 (NIV)

I LOVE THAT THESE POWERFUL verses about hope come at the end of the passage that begins with creation "groaning as in the pains of childbirth" (Romans 8:22, NIV). As the mother of two precious sons, I find it a sweetly suitable way to start my Advent reflections. Now more than ever, I and the world groan as we wait patiently or otherwise.

I can't help but think of Mary, the mother of Jesus, in her last few weeks of pregnancy. I wondered if she had impatient, groaning discomforts, magnified by the less-than-optimal condition of traveling during Jesus's world-shaping arrival.

Was she visualizing Gabriel's promises (Luke 1:30–33)? Could she be remembering the inspired hope of her Magnificat (Luke 1:46–55)? Was she worried about the pains of childbirth or was she longing to cuddle her newborn? Was she imagining a mysterious future as mother to the Messiah?

There's no way for me to know much more about the thoughts and feelings of Mary than the Bible states, but I know this: every hope is ultimately fulfilled by Jesus's arrival, first as the world-changing gift of love born in human form and second as a conquering King who will make everything—everything—right (Revelations 19:16). As I enter this season of Advent, I vow to groan less, wait patiently, and hope expectantly for what is to come. —ISABELLA CAMPOLATTARO

FAITH STEP: *List a few things you're hoping for today. Pray about each one until Christmas, in the name of Jesus, our ultimate Hope.*

First Sunday of Advent, December 1

May the God of hope fill you with all joy and peace as you trust in him, so that you may overflow with hope by the power of the Holy Spirit. Romans 15:13 (NIV)

I HAD SPENT MORE THAN a decade in a spiritually abusive church. One of the many things members were required to abstain from was Christmas. Marrying and moving several states away from that church helped me to unpack the myriad of unhealthy mental patterns that were knotted up in my head. It didn't happen overnight. It was a slow progression of God renewing my mind, day by day, and helping me to find true hope and freedom in Christ.

A few years into this deconstructing process, I was shopping at the mall during the Christmas season. Holiday vendors had set up their pop-up booths selling everything from personalized ornaments to embroidered stockings. I approached a booth and perused the ornaments. A little red sled with two shiny snowflakes caught my eye. I bought it, asked the attendant to personalize it with my name and the year and brought it home. It was a step of hope.

Hope that Jesus really did love me. Hope that all of the brokenness from my life, up to that point, could be redeemed. Hope that one of the darkest seasons of my life I've ever walked through was finally coming to a close.

Years later, I hang that little red sled on my Christmas tree and thank Jesus for being the God of hope and for setting me free.
—KRISTEN WEST

FAITH STEP: *Peruse your ornaments and choose one that inspires hope. Place it in a prominent place as a reminder to hope in Jesus.*

Monday, December 2

---

*Therefore let us not judge one another anymore, but rather
resolve this, not to put a stumbling block or a cause to fall in our
brother's way. Romans 14:13 (NKJV)*

TODAY I AM BAKING *hildabrötchen.* These German shortbread sandwich cookies are filled with jam and topped with powdered sugar. They are time-consuming and difficult to prepare but well worth the effort—my husband's favorite. One of the reasons I make them for my holiday platter is that my mother did, and before that her mother did, and so on. I suspect that when I'm gone, my daughter will take up the tradition.

My mother shied away from the American measurement system. She chose her metric scale. I use cups and teaspoons. The result is the same cookie, but with slight differences, due to our preferences. I can only guess the changes my daughter might make to the original recipe.

Faith is like that. It's said that if you ask ten believers about heaven, you'll receive ten different answers. Just as the subtle changes to my family's Christmas cookies reflect our individuality, each of us sees Jesus from our own unique perspective.

Like these challenging treats, at times we'll face unexpected trials. We'll deal with them in our specific way, according to our personal history and personalities. And we'll rest in the knowledge that we are not alone. We have Jesus. He is the one vital ingredient to all our beliefs.

Like those delicious sandwich cookies, knowing Jesus is so sweet.
—HEIDI GAUL

FAITH STEP: *Pull out a long-forgotten family recipe and make it for loved ones. Be sure to add a bit of your individual taste to the dish.*

MONDAY, DECEMBER 2

But just as he who called you is holy, so be holy in all you do.
1 Peter 1:15 (NIV)

"I LOVE THIS MOVIE!" MY son, Mason, exclaimed when *Elf* lit up our television screen. With our family huddled together under blankets on the couch, the white tree lights twinkled and a fire danced in the fireplace. I realized *Elf* means so much more to us than just a funny Christmas film. It's our annual tradition that marks the start of the holiday season. As the hustle and bustle of December begins, we stop, come together, and literally connect, shoulders touching shoulders. It takes so little effort, yet we're blessed. We're blessed by the presence of the other, and we're blessed because we take notice: we recognize the bond that connects us, making us a family while the movie plays. It's another fiber weaving its way around our hearts, binding us closer to each other.

That's what time together does. Whether we're having deep conversation, playing silly games, or sitting quietly together on the couch, it's not the activity that matters; it's the time spent together that deepens the relationship.

So too it is with Jesus. Whether we're shopping for the perfect present, elbow deep in flour while making cookie dough, or leaning over the table wrapping gifts, when we invite Jesus into our holiday preparations, our tasks become holy. They also become more fibers weaving their way around our hearts, binding us closer to Him.
—CLAIRE MCGARRY

FAITH STEP: *What tradition brings you closer to Jesus? If you can't think of one, pray to be inspired with something that will deepen your relationship with Him.*

Monday, December 2

You, Lord, keep my lamp burning; my God turns my darkness into light. Psalm 18:28 (NIV)

The lights of Christmas. What joy they bring! Except while I was grieving. When our three-year-old son Blake died suddenly from an illness, two months before Christmas, those cheerful lights mocked a deep inner darkness of my soul. My husband, Jeff, and I decorated a Christmas tree for our two surviving sons, but it was too painful for us to adorn the outside with our customary display of lights. Ours was the only unlit house in the neighborhood, accurately reflecting the bleakness in our hearts.

Time passed. To reclaim a sense of normalcy for our children, we resumed our outside lighting displays. Two decades later, on the Christmas following the loss of our infant grandson Welles, we again refrained from displaying our outside lights, to spare Welles's parents the pain we'd experienced so many years before. Instead, we planted a small oak in our back yard to commemorate Welles's life and strung some tiny white lights on the tree. When Christmas was over, we found we couldn't bear to take the lights down. Those tiny white lights gave us hope and reminded us we would see Welles again.

Four Christmases have passed since we first decorated Welles's tree. The little oak has grown taller and fuller, and we've added more sets of tiny white lights. Now, every evening at dusk, the lights come on, illuminating the darkness. They shine until the sun rises, reminding us that Welles is with us still, in Jesus's tender care. —Pat Butler Dyson

---

Faith Step: *Carry a lighted candle into a darkened room. Observe what a remarkable difference the light makes. Then meditate on the difference Jesus, the Light of the World, makes in your life.*

TUESDAY, DECEMBER 3

For by grace you have been saved through faith. And this is not your own doing; it is the gift of God, not a result of works, so that no one may boast. Ephesians 2:8–9 (ESV)

IN DECEMBER, WHEN GLORIOUSLY COLORED leaves float about outdoors, I often wear my red, full-length coat to church and special events. It's the most beautiful coat I've ever owned, a gift from my husband, Michael. When I put it on, I feel his tender love envelop me like a warm blanket. A gift given because my husband loves me.

Often, I don my lovely, red paisley pashmina scarf, a present from my mother. Many mornings, I curl up in my comfy bed with a cup of coffee, reading from the Bible my father gave me for Christmas when I was a college freshman. Gifts given because I'm their daughter and they love me.

Many cherished baubles adorn our home that were given by dear friends or family. We share a relationship. We know or love each other.

God also gave me a gift, His one and only Son, Jesus. Unlike my coat, scarf, baubles or even my Bible, the gift of Jesus is eternal. The givers of my earthly gifts have given me tokens of their love that I earned through a relationship. But Jesus's gift of salvation is offered to me, and to everyone, freely, without merit—all we have to do is believe and receive. And why? Solely because Jesus loves me and wants a relationship with me. He loves you too. —JENNIFER ANNE F. MESSING

FAITH STEP: *To accept the free gift of salvation that Jesus offers you, confess your sins and ask Him to come into your heart today.*

Tuesday, December 3

But when the right time came, God sent his Son, born of a woman, subject to the law. Galatians 4:4 (NLT)

WHEN I LEARNED THAT MY sister, Meghan, had gone into labor one December morning while I was at work, I kept my phone close and got updates from our parents. About 15 minutes before my lunch break, they called and said Meghan had changed her mind about having visitors in the delivery room, and if I got there in time, she would let me witness the birth of my niece.

I grabbed my purse, yelled an apology to my boss, and ran out the door, keeping my parents on the phone as I sped down the freeway. I ran into the hospital like a crazy woman and found my sister's room just in time to see my niece, Lacy, arrive on the scene. It was by far the best lunch break I ever had, and I knew only God could have orchestrated perfect timing like that.

I think about His perfect timing during Advent when I consider the birth of Jesus. I always knew His birth was special because of what happened and how it happened, but it was also special because of *when* it happened. For centuries, it seemed as if God was silent or absent. But while His people felt forgotten or abandoned, He was actually readying the world to receive His Son. When all the plans were in place and the world was finally ready, the clock struck Christmas, and Jesus was born! —EMILY E. RYAN

FAITH STEP: *Research the "intertestamental period" to learn what was happening in the world before the birth of Jesus. As you see evidence of the Lord's perfect timing, reflect on His timing in your own life.*

TUESDAY, DECEMBER 3

*So the Lord himself will give you this sign: A virgin will become
pregnant and give birth to a son, and she will name him Immanuel
[God Is With Us]. Isaiah 7:14 (GW)*

A FEW YEARS AGO, OUR family added *The Man Who Invented Christmas*
to our holiday watchlist. One of my favorite scenes shows Charles
Dickens struggling to name his main character before he begins to
write the story. The maids overhear him mumbling and shouting:
"Tightfisted miser…Scrounger! Covetous old sinner…Scrabbly…
Scrimple…Scrunge!" Dickens explains to a maid, "Get the name
right and then, if you're lucky, the character will appear. He's not
here yet." After she leaves, he suddenly shouts "Scrooge!" Dickens
turns to see the perfect image of his character, whom he argues and
converses with throughout the writing of *A Christmas Carol*.

Before the creation of the world, God wrote His story of salvation
and redemption for the human race. He made sure to get the main
character's name just right and shared it ahead of time. Through the
prophet Isaiah, God explained that one day He would come to earth
in human form and live among His people. Centuries later, an angel
declared that Mary's son would be named Jesus, or Savior, because
He would save people from their sins (Matthew 1:21, AMPC).

I love that the Bible gives many other names for Jesus, including
Wonderful Counselor (Isaiah 9:6), Light of the World (John 8:12),
and the True Vine (John 15:1). Each title teaches me more about
Jesus's character and His role in my life, helping me know Him
more fully. His titles also remind me why Jesus is the main character
in my personal story. —DIANNE NEAL MATTHEWS

FAITH STEP: *List a few of Jesus's names or titles that mean the most to you and
tell Him why.*

WEDNESDAY, DECEMBER 4

Now my eyes will be open and my ears attentive to the prayers offered in this place. 2 Chronicles 7:15 (NIV)

I FAKED A SMILE AS my husband told me his office would be transitioning to work-from-home in the new year. After months of praying for a way to fit everyone's differing needs into the planned renovation of our basement space, another request was not the solution I had in mind.

Busying myself in the kitchen, I heard an old Doug Stone lyric coming through the radio: "…love grows best in little houses, with fewer walls to separate…" The lighthearted song about family togetherness in a small home was a stark contrast to the tension our close quarters were creating. I'd hoped the planned winter renovation would ease the strain for our family, not increase it. A separate sewing room, painting space, and now two offices would be more than the area would allow. Could fewer walls be the answer?

After all, Jesus had to share His first home too. When Mary and Joseph entered Bethlehem, they were turned away time and again. With the moment of Jesus's birth imminent, an innkeeper took pity and offered them the only place available, a humble stable to share with animals. Not ideal, in my mind. Yet the small space was big enough to hold the greatest gift of all. God intentionally provided room for His only Son, showing the world that even a tiny floor plan could hold greatness and majesty. If the Holy Family could make a small space work, so could we. —GLORIA JOYCE

FAITH STEP: *Are you struggling with a project seemingly without a solution? Look with a different lens. Then ask yourself: What would Jesus do?*

WEDNESDAY, DECEMBER 4

You will be enriched in every way so that you can be generous on every occasion, and through us your generosity will result in thanksgiving to God. 2 Corinthians 9:11 (NIV)

AFTER A LITTLE PRODDING, I now have the Christmas wish lists from my grandkids. My, how things have changed. Yes, it's nice to have online purchasing links. And I'm grateful that the grands expressed their understanding that two or three families might have to pool resources to afford what they'd included on their lists.

My mind flew back several decades to the Christmas my sister and I had only one thing on our list. We'd been saving cereal box tops so we could each get a doll advertised on the snap-crackle-pop box. We were too young to know if we'd saved enough, but somehow we understood that finding the dolls under the Christmas tree wouldn't be a given but a true gift.

On Christmas Day, from our perpetually hardworking, perpetually strapped for cash, but also perpetually generous parents, we both received a doll plus a plastic carrying case with two more outfits and tiny plastic hangers.

We'd asked for one thing and received so much more.

In some ways, any celebration of Christmas will reflect God's "so much more." We needed a Savior. He sent a Savior who loved us. We needed redemption. The Christ child grew and eventually gave His last drop of blood to win it for us. We needed to know we were understood. Jesus proved He does. We needed to know we were accepted. He called us Beloved. We needed a forever Home. Jesus handed us the keys. —CYNTHIA RUCHTI

FAITH STEP: *Show extreme generosity to someone in need this Christmas in a way that reveals Christ's provision, not yours.*

WEDNESDAY, DECEMBER 4

"I have come into the world as a light, so that no one who believes in me should stay in darkness." John 12:46 (NIV)

I LOVE LIGHTS, AND HOLIDAY lights for the Christmas season are my favorite. I love driving through neighborhoods on wintry nights and seeing rooftops, windows, lawns, and trees all set aglow on a city block. What's usually a dark, cold, and lifeless strip of road for more than 300 days in a year is transformed by light.

The festive energy my dad had when I was a kid is one of the reasons holiday lights are my favorite. Some of my earliest memories are centered around how he decorated for Christmas. Dad was producer and director of the holiday "show" in our house, meticulously setting each string of lights in its proper place. The blinking lights transformed our living room into a magical space. At night, I would sit on our couch as often (and as long) as I could soaking in the warm glow. I was always a little sad when we had to turn off the lights.

Today, I still get a little sad when it's time to turn off the Christmas lights in my house. Fortunately, I don't have to rely on those lights to feel like I'm in a magical space since Jesus, the Light of the World, lives within me. Because of His transformative light, I have the privilege of basking in His warm radiance all year long. His light will never turn off. It lasts forever. —ERICKA LOYNES

FAITH STEP: *Focus on the light used most in your house. Every time you turn it on or off, thank Jesus for His never-dimming light.*

THURSDAY, DECEMBER 5

My ears had heard of you but now my eyes have seen you. Job 42:5 (NIV)

OUR FAMILY HAS ENTERED THE season of college planning and visits, though I can hardly believe we're here. It's fun to dream with our teens and discover how Jesus is guiding their futures.

Living on the edge of this next season hits me with nostalgia. I've been sending old photos of the kids to our family text group and laughing with them over cute ways they pronounced words like "flahler" (flower) and "hoptopter" (helicopter). I'm happy to anticipate their new adventures but also a little sad to consider how life will change.

I feel this before-and-after juxtaposition: before they leave home, and afterward, when it will feel kind of empty. The changes of life can hold so many conflicting emotions.

Advent makes me thoughtful about the before-and-after reality of earthly life and eternity to come. Advent symbolizes the upcoming changes God was about to usher into the world through Jesus's birth, an event that marked a divine before and after in humanity's story. Before the first Advent, no one had heard of baby Jesus. But after He was born, our earthly story shifted from judgment and death to redemption and life eternal.

One day we will be free of conflicting emotions surrounding *befores* and *afters*. This season I want to soak up the importance of Advent and allow Jesus to prepare me before whatever He plans next, not only with my life but with my teens. —ERIN KEELEY MARSHALL

FAITH STEP: *Write a letter to Jesus asking Him to prepare you before the upcoming year. Seal the letter to read during Advent next year. Thank Him now for His guidance to come.*

THURSDAY, DECEMBER 5

*Your love is so extravagant, it reaches higher than the heavens! Your
faithfulness is so astonishing, it stretches to the skies! Psalm 108:4 (TPT)*

MY 13-YEAR-OLD GRANDSON PHENIXX STOOD in front of me and
pulled out a small, red stocking from behind his back. "Merry
Christmas, Grandma," he proclaimed.

I smiled with anticipation. This was the first time he had given
me a gift. I shook out the stocking to find $13.82.

"It's all the money I had in my piggybank, and I wanted you to
have it," said Phenixx sweetly.

My eyes welled up with tears as I gave him a bear hug that he's
probably still recovering from to this day. The rest of us had purchased gifts within our budgets or from our surplus. Not Phenixx.
His extravagant gift was completely and unreservedly sacrificial,
given with utter joy and cheer.

It was a timely reminder of God's most extravagant gift. The generosity and sacrificial heart of our Father gave Jesus to be born in
the flesh, walk the earth, navigate all the ups and downs of humanity, and, finally, die for our sins so we could be reconciled to God.

Jesus gave His all for us; should we offer any less? —KRISTEN WEST

FAITH STEP: *What extravagant gift can you offer someone this season?*

THURSDAY, DECEMBER 5

A true friend is always loyal, and a brother is born to help in time of need. Proverbs 17:17 (TLB)

FAMILY PROBLEMS I EXPERIENCED WHILE growing up have often made it difficult for me to make close friends. Decades ago, I became good friends with a woman from church named Linda. Unfortunately, we lost touch after our family changed churches.

Life in this new congregation was exciting, but I always missed Linda. We'd both grown up in the United States and a third-world country, were published authors, and moms of school-aged children. We had common interests in photography and scrapbooking. We clicked so easily, but without the ability to see each other on a regular basis at church, we drifted apart.

Naturally I've enjoyed many casual friendships and social media friendships, yet my heart yearns for a kindred spirit like Linda. A few years ago, in desperation, I asked Jesus to bring a new best friend into my life. But every time I thought I'd met that person, God moved her on.

So presently, during this season of waiting, as I pray daily and abide in Jesus's presence, He is filling me up with His everlasting, unconditional love so I can be vulnerable enough to trust someone again. God is also challenging me to be more friendly in social settings and transforming me into a faithful, loyal confidante, so I will be ready once my wait is over and I meet my new best friend. —JENNIFER ANNE F. MESSING

FAITH STEP: *Are you waiting for Jesus to bring a new friend into your life? Pray that He will give you skills to be best-friend-ready when the two of you meet.*

Friday, December 6

And she gave birth to her firstborn, a son. She wrapped him in cloths and placed him in a manger, because there was no guest room available for them. Luke 2:7 (NIV)

CHRISTMAS IS BY FAR MY favorite holiday, and I confess I decorate before Thanksgiving. I cherish my tree and ornaments, assorted indoor and outdoor décor, lights, greenery, wrappings and ribbons, but I love my mangers most. I have several pretty ones, but my treasure is a large Neapolitan Nativity. My parents were from Naples, Italy, famous for pizza, nearby Capri, Pompei, and Sorrento, and for the spectacular, elaborate Nativities found on Via San Gregorio Armeno.

Via San Gregorio Armeno is a sloped, narrow cobblestone street lined with small stores, some no bigger than a shed, with mangers and a vast assortment of figurines and landscape elements like palm trees, shrubs, fountains, boulders, stone, and stucco structures. They come in all styles and sizes, for any budget, and you could never run out of choices to expand your collection. I have many pieces.

Aside from the physical beauty of each element, I love how it represents the gritty, human, varied reality of ancient Bethlehem and its vicinity, with some poetic liberties. My crèche has the Holy Family, a shepherd, and wise men, along with a produce stand, fishmonger, families, and farmers. It's a vivid reminder that our Savior left the unparalleled perfection of heaven to come into our common, chaotic world. And why? He did it for love. —ISABELLA CAMPOLATTARO

FAITH STEP: *Imagine the Holy Family's journey to Bethlehem and Jesus's infancy in a busy town. Incorporate a few real-life details in your own manger if you're inspired.*

FRIDAY, DECEMBER 6

My comfort in my suffering is this: Your promise preserves my life.
Psalm 119:50 (NIV)

FIVE DAYS AFTER CHRISTMAS IN 2009, I received the phone call that is every parent's worst nightmare. Our 21-year-old son, Steven, had been killed in a car crash.

As I fell to my knees, I wept over his unwrapped presents still under the Christmas tree. He'd taken some gifts back to his apartment, but he'd left sweaters never to be worn and a beef stick, never to be eaten. How could God let this happen? I felt so alone.

Our church had just studied the lessons on Advent. I tried to remember we were living in the "between times" when Jesus was born and the time when He would return to earth as the conquering King (1 Thessalonians 4:16–17). I believed that I would someday see Steven again, but that didn't help much. I was so angry with God. Nothing comforted me.

Months passed and my grief did not get easier. To be honest, if one more person assured me Steven was in a better place, or they knew how I felt because their dog just died, I felt like I was going to lose it.

But that Advent lesson was not lost on me. We might be living in the between times, but the One who knew unjust suffering would never leave me to suffer alone. Jesus was right beside me.
—JEANNIE HUGHES

FAITH STEP: *Think of a situation when you felt alone in your suffering. Then think of a way Jesus was there, even if you didn't know it then.*

FRIDAY, DECEMBER 6

Then Jesus spoke to them again, saying, "I am the light of the world. He who follows Me shall not walk in darkness, but have the light of life." John 8:12 (NKJV)

I AM CLUMSY. IF SOME people are poetry in motion, I might resemble a limerick. But I don't mind. It's just another aspect of how Jesus designed me. Still, since I'm capable of tripping on air in broad daylight, I take precautions at night. Night-lights are spread throughout the house to guide my way in the darkness. I trust those tiny bulbs to get my sleepy self wherever I aim to go.

God's most precious gift—the Holy Child—came into our world in the quiet black of night. So God in His wisdom created the perfect night-light to find Jesus, a bright shining star. The first to follow it were shepherds and their flocks. Matthew 2:2 mentions wise men making a journey from the East, trusting in the star to lead them to our Lord.

I'm no astronomer. I don't know whether that heavenly light still glows in the sky. But that's okay. As a believer, I have a different Light to guide my way. Jesus. Will I trip along life's way? Maybe. But I trust Jesus's light will help me reach my eternal destination, where I will rest in the glow of His love forever. —HEIDI GAUL

FAITH STEP: *Tonight, take in the vast beauty of the night sky. Meditate on those who made the journey in the light of that one special star, and give thanks for the blessing of knowing Jesus, the Light of the World.*

SATURDAY, DECEMBER 7

For every creature of God is good, and nothing is to be refused if
it is received with thanksgiving. 1 Timothy 4:4 *(NKJV)*

A FEW DAYS BEFORE CHRISTMAS, my daughters Melissa and Brooke and my grandson Winston burst into my bedroom, yelling, "Merry Christmas!" In Winston's arms was a tiny black kitten, swathed in a huge red ribbon.

"Oh, no!" I cried. "I don't want another cat!" I'd lost my beloved old cat Tux months before. I was still grieving him and not ready to open my heart yet.

"But, Mom," Melissa said, "I know you're lonely because you feed the stray cats at Walgreens every day. You need a cat and this poor little guy needs a home."

"Not *every* day," I corrected, "and besides, haven't you heard it's a bad idea to surprise a person with a pet? I don't have cat food or a litter box or any items a cat needs!" The merry cat-gifters assured me they had taken care of everything.

All day long, I agonized over the kitten. I agreed to let him stay overnight in the utility room, but in the morning, he'd have to go. My daughter told me Winston went to bed crying.

Sleepless, I prayed, *Jesus, what do I do?* This kitten was my kids' gift to me because they love me and they want me to be happy. The kitten needs a home. I *have* a home and I adore cats. I felt Jesus's nudge: open your heart.

The next morning, I talked to Winston. "How about we name him Kris Kringle?" —PAT BUTLER DYSON

FAITH STEP: *Take a moment and ponder what Jesus is calling you to open your heart to this Advent season.*

SATURDAY, DECEMBER 7

For God did not send his Son into the world to condemn the world, but to save the world through him. John 3:17 (NIV)

I RECENTLY LEARNED THAT THE comic book hero Superman was created when World War II was brewing in Europe. That superhero was a way to encourage people not to lose hope in the face of all that unrest.

World War II may be behind us now, but we're all experiencing our own personal battles: combating an illness, fighting to pay the mortgage, sparring with a loved one. These conflicts don't disappear just because it's Advent. Even if things aren't that dire, the chaos and demands of the season can feel like an unrelenting onslaught of have-to's and expectations, leaving one exhausted. Finding peace and being made right with God is something we can't do ourselves.

That's why Jesus was born. He didn't come with a cape, however. He was wrapped in swaddling clothes and placed in a manger, surrounded by animals and hay. At first glance, there didn't appear to be anything super or heroic about this innocent Child. Yet the Bible explains that He came down to lift us up, conquering the enemy for good and saving all of humanity from the grasp of original sin.

Advent is a reminder that our Superhero, Jesus, has come to save us. All we need to do is believe in Him, hand over our burdens, and let Him rescue us from it all. —CLAIRE MCGARRY

FAITH STEP: *Reflect over your life and compile a list of the times when Jesus rescued you as no other superhero could have. Give thanks for each and every time.*

SATURDAY, DECEMBER 7

Wait for the LORD; be strong and take heart and wait for the LORD.
Psalm 27:14 *(NIV)*

THE FIRST WEEKEND IN NOVEMBER, my home gets transformed from its regular, run-of-the-mill, everyday house into a Christmas wonderland. I wake up giddy with excitement, fling open the attic door, and begin hauling Christmas boxes, totes, and cubbies out of storage. Before long, my foyer and living room are littered with ornaments, garland, and baubles galore.

As Michael Bublé croons in the background, I meticulously place Christmas décor in the entryway and hallway passages, wrap strands of lights neatly around the tree, and plug in the balsam fir air fresheners. Halfway through the transformation, I grab my water bottle (this level of hard work requires much hydration), take a seat in my living room, and admire my handiwork as I anticipate what I have yet to do. In the ambiance of the softly lit tree, I prepare my heart with expectancy for what Jesus might do during this special season. What new insight might He show me this year about the significance of this holy season? How might He use me to touch the life of someone else in an eternally impactful way? Where does my heart need to be softened and molded to look more like Jesus, my beautiful Savior and King?

I wait for Him.
Expectantly.
Humbly.
With anticipation.

Christmas is the season to fix my gaze on Jesus with excitement and gratitude for what He has done. And to wait with eager expectation for all that He has yet to do. —KRISTEN WEST

FAITH STEP: *Find a quiet place and ponder what Jesus has done in your life. Pray about what you are waiting for Him to do.*

PEACE

God of Peace, at the first Christmas
Your angel announced, "Glory to God
in the highest heaven, and on earth
peace to those on whom His favor rests"
(Luke 2:14, NIV). Thank You for the peace
Jesus promised, not as the world gives,
but willing, deep, and abiding peace.

Grant that we may live at peace with
everyone, making every effort to do what
leads to peace. Let the peace of Christ rule
in our hearts, now and forever. Amen.

SECOND SUNDAY OF ADVENT, DECEMBER 8

Since we have been made right in God's sight by faith,
we have peace with God because of what Jesus Christ our
Lord has done for us. Romans 5:1 *(NLT)*

DURING DECEMBER I SEE AND hear the expression "peace on earth" everywhere: in carols and holiday plays, on decorations and Christmas cards. Those words can seem out of place when I look around at our culture or watch news about current events. The phrase can feel jarring when I'm at odds with a family member or neighbor, or struggling with inner turmoil. In those moments, I need to remember why Jesus is called the Prince of Peace.

The message of Christmas is that Jesus was born to take away the sin that separated us from God. As a follower of Jesus, I'm called to strive to live at peace with others (Romans 12:18). He wants me to be ready to forgive or apologize when needed, extending grace to others just as I've received grace from Him (Colossians 3:13). Jesus also invites me to cast all my cares on Him and live free of guilt, regrets, and poor self-esteem (1 Peter 5:7). For me, this inner peace is the hardest to achieve. I'm learning to extend grace to myself and live in the assurance of His unconditional love.

Prince of Peace is a fitting title for Jesus. He shows me how to have peace with God the Father, with other people, and with myself. Regardless of what is happening around me or within me, I can embrace the peace that goes beyond my human understanding (Philippians 4:7). —DIANNE NEAL MATTHEWS

FAITH STEP: *What relationship in your life lacks peace? Ask Jesus to reveal how you can be reconciled with God, another person, or yourself.*

SECOND SUNDAY OF ADVENT, DECEMBER 8

---

*"Look! The virgin will conceive a child! She will give birth to a son,
and they will call him Immanuel, which means 'God is with us.'"*
Matthew 1:23 (NLT)

IN THE PAST FEW MONTHS, my 20-pound cat, Wally, has developed an endearing habit. When I sit in my usual seat at our dining table, Wally leaps onto the chair beside me and puts his huge paw on my leg. If I stand up to fetch a spoon or a condiment, the minute I sit back down that paw reaches out again. My three cats are mainly couch decorations, but when Wally connects with me like that, I feel as if he's saying, "I am here for you."

When Jesus came to earth in the flesh, He was God's announcement to us: "I am here for you." Jesus's very name means "God is with us."

Knowing that God is with me every minute fills my heart with tremendous peace. No power or evil can steal me from Jesus (John 10:28). Jesus has authority over everything and everyone (Colossians 1:15–18). No matter where I go, Jesus is with me (Psalm 139:7–10). Jesus calls me "friend" (John 15:14–15). And Jesus constantly prays for me (Hebrews 7:25).

The Father didn't send Jesus to earth only to die as our Savior and rise again as our King. He also sent Jesus to be our constant companion, our Immanuel, God with us. Which means a thousand times more to me than Wally's paw on my knee. —JEANETTE LEVELLIE

FAITH STEP: *Look up one of the scriptures above and ponder the truth of "Immanuel, God with us."*

SECOND SUNDAY OF ADVENT, DECEMBER 8

The Lord gives strength to his people; the Lord blesses
his people with peace. Psalm 29:11 (NIV)

STARING AT THE STARS IN my backyard while the fire pit flickered to life, I was weary and unsettled. It was a mild December, a rarity in the Northeast. Restless, I sent a spontaneous text to friends that brought them to our home. The quiet gathering was just what I needed to boost my mood. Turns out, I wasn't the only one.

Several of us were in difficult situations, including caregiving for an elderly parent, blindsided by divorce, challenging dynamics at work, family infighting. I wasn't the only one who longed for a tranquil get-together and an opportunity for group support within an emotional winter. As I stoked the fire, someone had the idea to pray together, calling Jesus to join us in our suffering. *Why hadn't I thought of that?*

As I sat alone following everyone's departure, I felt peace for the first time in a while. Holding tight to Jesus's hand, the embers in my heart for Him were uncovered and I finally felt contentment during this holy season. The gathering didn't take away the emotions weighing me down. But the warmth of friendship, combined with Jesus's tender mercies, added another log to my inner fire, flaming not my own peace but His to keep me going. —GLORIA JOYCE

FAITH STEP: *Do you need refueling or know someone struggling this holiday season? Spend time with a friend today by phone or in person. Invite Jesus too. Lean on each other and share the warmth and peace He provides.*

MONDAY, DECEMBER 9

But those who wait on the LORD shall renew their strength; they shall mount up with wings like eagles, they shall run and not be weary, they shall walk and not faint. Isaiah 40:31 (NKJV)

I LIVE IN HILL COUNTRY. Think Appalachia, but in Arkansas. My house on a hill overlooks the Arkansas River. I love to watch the seasons change from my deck, but winter presents a challenge for me with its bleakness. As leaves fall and the landscape becomes grayer, I tend to feel my own soul wither with it. I might be better off if I could hibernate, but alas, I am not a bear. I have responsibilities.

The consolation nature offers during winters here is bald eagles. I realized I had come to live among them the winter after we built our house. One December I went to my deck. Below me in a treetop, a magnificent eagle was roosting. Against the dull backdrop of a muddy river and bare trees its great white head shone in the sun.

As it took flight, I gasped and was reminded that Jesus is with me. What a comfort to know I can draw from His strength and light in every season. And, just like that eagle, Jesus often shows up in the bleakest and most unexpected places. —GWEN FORD FAULKENBERRY

FAITH STEP: *As an adventure, see if there is a place nearby where you can observe bald eagles. If none are available, watch a YouTube video of eagles in flight. Remember this is the word picture Isaiah provided for us—we who wait on the Lord Jesus. This is who we are with His wind beneath our wings.*

MONDAY, DECEMBER 9

*"Simply put, if you're not willing to take what is dearest to you,
whether plans or people, and kiss it good-bye, you can't be my disciple."*
Luke 14:33 (MSG)

FOR THE FOURTH CONSECUTIVE YEAR, my husband, son, and I have stayed home for Christmas, and not spent time with relatives or close friends that day. It's a practice we started during the pandemic. As much as I have missed the exciting, sometimes frantic, pace of traveling, shopping, and interacting with relatives and friends, I have enjoyed the deliberate pause during the holiday these past few years.

Last year's stay-at-home Christmas felt even more different than the previous ones, because my husband and son didn't want to exchange gifts. I'm a bit embarrassed to say my gift list was (and is always) long, but I decided to follow their example. Instead, we prioritized charitable giving, attended a special Christmas Eve church service, and gave gifts only to a few relatives and close friends. On Christmas Day, the three of us spent time in prayer and the Word, and later enjoyed a movie—a favorite family pastime. I was surprised I didn't mourn the absence of presents, as I thought I might.

Before bed, I planted my feet firmly on the floor of our living room, closed my eyes, and thanked Jesus for a wonderful day. Christmas with no gifts made for one of the strangest yet most satisfying holidays. Ridding myself of unwrapping new items under the tree made room for me to receive what was most important that day. Truly, the magic of Christmas was not the presents but in Jesus's presence. —ERICKA LOYNES

FAITH STEP: *Think about ways you could change it up this season to experience less tradition and more Jesus.*

MONDAY, DECEMBER 9

For God, who said, "Let light shine out of the darkness," made his light shine in our hearts to give us the light of the knowledge of God's glory displayed in the face of Christ. 2 Corinthians 4:6 (NIV)

ONE OF THE CANDLES IN my Advent wreath must be coated with some synthetic material. When I light the wick, the edges also catch on fire. It makes the flame absolutely brilliant, fierce, and radiant. But the wax burns at such a rate, it pours down the edges of the candle. In no time at all, that candle will be a wax stub, burnt out and useless.

I've had Advents like that. I'd shoot for the stars with my plans: cramming my calendar with fun activities, going big with my decorating and baking, and being on fire with the joy of the season. Oh, did I shine bright! Until I didn't. Inevitably, I'd burn up and burn out.

Keeping the glitz as my focus, my approach became synthetic and secular. The reason for the season isn't for me to shine bright. It's to look to the Light and let His grace illuminate my life. While I was busy making my exterior ready for Christmas, Jesus wanted me to open my heart so He could make my interior ready to celebrate His birth.

This year, I'm extinguishing my own brightness, quieting my soul, stepping into Jesus's presence and letting Him fire me up from within. That's the way to purify my spirit and prepare my heart for the Flame of Righteousness to be born. —CLAIRE MCGARRY

FAITH STEP: *Instead of lighting candles tonight, turn off the lights and sit for a moment with the Light of the World. Let Jesus illuminate you from within.*

TUESDAY, DECEMBER 10

On coming to the house, they saw the child with his mother Mary,
and they bowed down and worshiped him. Then they
opened their treasures and presented him with gifts of gold,
frankincense and myrrh. Matthew 2:11 (NIV)

ONE OF MY FAVORITE CHRISTMAS songs is "The Little Drummer Boy," which tells the fictional story of a child who meets baby Jesus shortly after He is born. The boy wishes he had something fabulous to give Jesus like the valuable gifts of gold, frankincense, and myrrh brought by the wise men, but because he's poor, he has nothing like that to offer. However, instead of focusing on what he doesn't have to give, the boy focuses on what he does have to give. He has a drum, so he uses that drum to play a song for Jesus.

Every time I hear that song, I let it remind me how the Lord has a unique purpose for my life (Jeremiah 29:11). I don't have to write like *that* author, or speak like *that* teacher, or parent like *that* mom. Like the Little Drummer Boy, I focus on what I have, rather than what I lack, and worship Jesus with all that I am. If all I have is a drum—or a pen, or a voice, or a house, or a dollar—then I'll let that be my offering to the One who is worthy. —EMILY E. RYAN

FAITH STEP: *Use a talent, possession, or skill to give Jesus a gift this holiday season.*

TUESDAY, DECEMBER 10

Christ had no sin, but God made him become sin so that in Christ we could become right with God. 2 Corinthians 5:21 (NCV)

EVERY DECEMBER DURING MY CHILDHOOD, my dad and brothers cut down a young cedar tree on our little farm. These trees didn't have the best shape, and it was hard to hang ornaments from the feathery branches. But the first Christmas after my marriage, I asked my parents to bring us one. As their car warmed up during the one-hour drive to our apartment, spiders began crawling out of the tree lying on the back seat. My husband, Richard, and I later discovered a bird's nest in the branches. Hardly perfect.

After we moved away, I spent a lot of time searching for the most perfectly shaped Christmas trees each year. Sometimes I felt intimidated by my friends' trendy or color-coordinated schemes. But I loved decorating with the ornaments we had collected and treasured through the years. I did, however, do a lot of snipping and rearranging of the branches when my obsessive-compulsive tendencies kicked in.

Through the years, I've learned to accept imperfections as a needed reminder: I am not perfect, but my Savior is. Instead of trying to create a flawless Christmas tree, I want to focus on Jesus, who perfectly decorates my life every day with His blessings. —DIANNE NEAL MATTHEWS

FAITH STEP: *Are you struggling with perfectionism this Christmas season? Intentionally do something imperfect to your tree to remind yourself of the One who is perfect.*

TUESDAY, DECEMBER 10

But after he had considered this, an angel of the Lord appeared
to him in a dream and said, "Joseph son of David, do not be afraid
to take Mary home as your wife, because what is conceived
in her is from the Holy Spirit." Matthew 1:20 (NIV)

BESIDES BEING A PASTOR, MY husband, Kevin, is also a music composer who's written thousands of songs. One year Kevin wrote a song titled "The Spirit of Christmas Is the Holy Spirit." Until I listened to his lyrics, I'd never realized the huge role the Holy Spirit played in Jesus's birth.

I knew the Holy Spirit was the one by whom Mary conceived. But His role in the advent of Christ only started there.

Thousands of years before Jesus came to earth, the Holy Spirit spoke through godly people to prophesy the coming of the Messiah. The Holy Spirit's power caused the perfect timing of the Christ child's birth (Galatians 4:4). I believe the Holy Spirit was the one who lit up the sky with glory when the baby destined to change darkness to light was born. Surely the Holy Spirit helped guide the shepherds through the night to the stable where Jesus—the bread from heaven—lay tucked in a feeding trough.

And the Holy Spirit is still at work today. As He did for Mary, the Holy Spirit helps us trust God when we receive an impossible assignment. As He reassured Joseph, the Holy Spirit gives us courage to step out in faith. And like a nurturing shepherd, the Holy Spirit guides us to our Good Shepherd, Jesus. That's something to sing about! —JEANETTE LEVELLIE

FAITH STEP: *Ask Jesus to help you see where the Holy Spirit is at work in your life.*

WEDNESDAY, DECEMBER 11

Peace I leave with you; my peace I give you. I do not give to you as the world gives. Do not let your hearts be troubled and do not be afraid. John 14:27 (NIV)

THE PROMISE OF PEACE SEEMS impossible in a world where peace and serene circumstances are in short supply. Yet I can say with honesty and wonder that because of Jesus, I've experienced peace and fearlessness that defy explanation. The birth of my son Isaac with Down syndrome is a prime example.

After a very hard time conceiving my first son, Pierce, I found myself unexpectedly pregnant at 43. I was honestly delighted and had no misgivings until my 12-week sonogram.

Moments into the exam, the sonogram technician's face fell, and she quickly excused herself to fetch my obstetrician. My heart skipped a beat, but then I was enveloped in an inexplicable calm. When my doctor entered and scrutinized the screen herself, she too looked somber. She invited me to join her in her office. That's when she told me there were several markers for a genetic anomaly.

She explained that further testing would confirm a diagnosis. I promptly declined, knowing we'd never terminate a pregnancy. When Isaac was born and the Down syndrome diagnosis was confirmed, I was heartbroken, angry, and scared, even though I treasured Isaac.

I sought Jesus as never before, begging for comfort, even as I nursed and cradled Isaac. Eventually, with a suddenness I cannot explain, peace swept over me once again.

Baby Jesus was the Prince of a peace that didn't exist before He came. Baby Isaac also proved to be a priceless gift of joy and love I couldn't anticipate until Jesus's perfect peace intervened. This object lesson has multiplied my faith to face anything since with greater peace. —ISABELLA CAMPOLATTARO

FAITH STEP: *Write down the people or circumstances that trouble you. Have a ceremony of giving each one to Jesus stating: I give you _____ and receive Your perfect peace.*

WEDNESDAY, DECEMBER 11

There are different kinds of gifts, but the same Spirit distributes them.
There are different kinds of service, but the same Lord.
1 Corinthians 12:4-5 (NIV)

CUDDLING UNDER A BLANKET WITH a book during our first snowstorm in almost two years, I stopped reading to glance out my frost-covered window. A warm mug in hand, I savored the beauty of the newly fallen snow, coating the world in icy white. As I slowly sipped an uninterrupted cuppa, my husband, Matt, alternatively was a flurry of activity. His office closed for the day, he'd already shoveled our walk, completed two indoor home repairs, and tidied our home office…all before lunch! What I viewed as a day to rest and revitalize before hosting for the upcoming holiday, Matt saw as a bonus day to catch up on chores.

Winter has a way of highlighting our unique personalities, bringing out the hibernating bear in me, while Matt scurries about like a squirrel unaffected by the seasons. Yet after 25 years of marriage, I know it is our differences that balance our union. Perhaps that is why the contemplative Advent and the bustling Christmas are a perfect pair. Calm and serene, abundant and joyful, the twosome intertwines in their own way to strengthen our faith. After all, Jesus made us unique in His own image. Jesus knows the quiet peace of Advent is a perfect complement to rejuvenate our spirit as we hurry about to prepare to jubilantly celebrate His birth.

Energized by the respite snow day, I'm ready to embrace Christmas with a bear hug! —GLORIA JOYCE

FAITH STEP: *Take a moment today to slow down and savor the Advent season. Whether in adoration or contemplation, have a cup of tea (or coffee) with Jesus.*

WEDNESDAY, DECEMBER 11

Though I sit in darkness, the LORD will be my light. Micah 7:8 (NIV)

I TWIST IN THE NEW bulb and turn the lamp switch. Light glows through the shade and drapes the space by the front window, and I draw in a breath and exhale peace. As the temperature slips lower in December, I want all the vibes of a warm haven.

For me, decorative lamps are key elements of that ambience. There's my silver one with a hot-pink shade I snagged for a dollar at a yard sale, and the two Target finds for my office and entry tables. And there's an old black one with the shade I embellished on our dining room buffet, a beachy one upstairs, and a cut-glass mini lamp on the kitchen counter.

It's fitting that Advent—the preparation for Jesus—is symbolized by candles and lights, and that it falls at the beginning of winter, when daylight hours wane to their fewest. Light has sacred roots loaded with holy meaning (Genesis 1:3–5). Jesus called Himself the light of the world (John 8:12), present before Creation (John 1:1–5).

When my lamps glow during the cozy first weeks of winter, my spirit settles into Advent. In a few weeks, December will reach its close, and God will gift the world with a little more light each day.

It's beautiful, the marvel of light. In the myriad ways Jesus reveals His light, He encourages me to look for Him, to prepare to see Him afresh during this Advent season. —ERIN KEELEY MARSHALL

FAITH STEP: *Consider adding a decorative lamp to your Christmas décor. Let its glow remind you of Jesus's light.*

Thursday, December 12

Thank God for this gift too wonderful for words! 2 Corinthians 9:15 *(NLT)*

My possessive cat, Pokey, pushed aside presents under our Christmas tree to find the perfect napping spot. Since we added gifts often, this was a constant challenge to Pokey. Seeing her rummage through packages reminded me of the time we tried something different one December 25th.

On Christmas morning, our six-year-old daughter, Esther, and three-year-old son, Ron, began to grab a gift from beneath the tree, rip the paper off, say "thank you," and then snatch another gift. What my husband, Kevin, and I planned as a fun celebration of Jesus ended up as a greed-fest. I was frustrated.

"Next year, what if we opened gifts on the twenty-sixth, like the British do?" I suggested the following day. "So we can focus on Jesus for His birthday." Kevin agreed.

When we warned the kids, several months in advance, they were not amused. We steeled ourselves against their whining and remained steadfast.

That Christmas morning, Kevin and I asked the Lord to help us honor Him throughout His birthday. We had a special breakfast of cinnamon rolls, took the kids to the sparsely populated park, and played board games after our traditional Christmas dinner. Amazingly, we never rushed anything. At the end of the day, we all agreed it was the most peaceful Christmas ever.

The following morning, Esther and Ron took their time opening gifts, examining and enthusing over each present before going on to the next one.

Although at first I suspected they feared a rerun of the giftless Christmas, they've continued their peaceful habit to this day.
—Jeanette Levellie

Faith Step: *Pray to be inspired for a new, Jesus–filled Christmas tradition.*

Thursday, December 12

"Come to me, all you who are weary and burdened, and I will give you rest." Matthew 11:28 (NIV)

WHEN I SAW MY FRIEND Betsy wearing a cute Christmas sweatshirt with the words: "The weary world rejoices," I immediately recognized the line from my favorite Christmas hymn, "O Holy Night." I'd sung the song hundreds of times over the years but had never let the weight of that particular line sink into my soul. Now that the simple lyrics were isolated from the rest of the song, it pierced my heart differently than it had before.

Weary is not a word I often hear others use or use myself. I might say I'm tired, worn out, exhausted, or sleepy, but seldom do I claim to be weary. And yet, when used to describe the state of the world, there are times when *weary* seems to fit quite well. The world was certainly weary when Jesus entered into it as a baby. Government oppression, political conflicts, religious unrest, widespread poverty. No wonder the people longed for a leader to rescue them from their weariness. But Jesus didn't overthrow political corruption or bring peace through public policies. Instead, He offered rest, peace, and joy through a relationship with Him.

When I watch the news, I feel like the word *weary* could be an appropriate description for the state of the world today as well. But instead of feeling burdened and hopeless, I remember Jesus and the rest He still offers. It's certainly worth rejoicing—for the weary world and for the weary soul. —EMILY E. RYAN

FAITH STEP: *Write a letter to Jesus expressing how you are feeling weary. Then write out the words of Matthew 11:28 and Isaiah 40:31 as His answer to your prayer.*

THURSDAY, DECEMBER 12

He is the image of the invisible God, the firstborn of all creation....
And he is before all things, and in him all things hold together.
Colossians 1:15, 17 (ESV)

THE CHURCH WHERE I GREW up had beautiful banners with the biblical names of Jesus on them. I used to sit in church, gaze at them, and memorize each name: Image of the Invisible God; Alpha and Omega; Rose of Sharon; Light of the World; Bread of Life; The Way, The Truth, and The Life; The Door; The Word; Prince of Peace; Wonderful; Counselor; Messiah; Lion of Judah; Lamb of God; Son of God; Son of Man; High Priest; King of Kings; Lord of Lords; Teacher. But after all these years, the one name that has come to mean the most to me is Immanuel: God with us.

I think it's because out of all Jesus is—and He truly is everything— the most important aspect of His character is that He is present. He is here. With us.

What would it mean if Jesus had all those other names but was not with us? The miracle of Christmas is that this being, this divine cosmic force, chose to put on human skin, live on earth, and reside in the hearts of all who know Him. That means you and I are never alone in this human experience. And there are no words to describe the magnificent wonder of that. —GWEN FORD FAULKENBERRY

FAITH STEP: *Write your favorite name of Jesus and hang it on your Christmas tree to remind you who He is.*

Friday, December 13

Where can I go from your Spirit? Where can I flee from your presence?
If I go up to the heavens, you are there; if I make my bed in the depths,
you are there. Psalm 139:7–8 (NIV)

LAST NOVEMBER, I RECEIVED A text asking for my address. I responded: *Hi, this message showed up on my laptop but not my phone, so it doesn't show any name. Who is this? (Sorry but I have to make sure you're not an ax murderer before I send my address.)* My longtime friend Paulette immediately responded with a laughing emoji and identified herself. I should have known.

Paulette and I became friends during the time my husband and I lived in Illinois. Later, job changes took us to four other states and shuffled us between apartments, temporary rentals, and houses. Paulette and I only communicated on social media, but each December I knew I'd receive a Christmas card from her along with a photo of her grandsons. It's been such a comfort to have a friend who keeps up with me, especially considering how often my address has changed.

These days I have fewer Christmas cards to display on my mantel, but I treasure the promise that Jesus is always close to me. He always knows where I am, not just geographically but emotionally and spiritually as well. It's such a comfort to have a Savior who keeps up with me more closely than even the best earthly friend does. —DIANNE NEAL MATTHEWS

FAITH STEP: *Read Psalm 139 and marvel at how intimately Jesus knows you. Record your favorite verses to keep as a reminder for times when you feel lonely or forgotten.*

FRIDAY, DECEMBER 13

One thing I ask from the LORD, this only do I seek: that I may dwell in the house of the LORD all the days of my life, to gaze on the beauty of the LORD and to seek him in his temple. Psalm 27:4 *(NIV)*

AT MY CHURCH LAST YEAR, Advent season was packed with a special week of prayer, a Night of Hope focused on healing, a Christmas concert for the public, a special movie screening, donations for The Giving Tree, and a Christmas Eve service. Though Advent is one of the most anticipated times of the year at my church—and for many Christians—observing it is a fairly new practice for me. I have often wondered why this reflective, liturgical tradition wasn't a part of my early church experience.

I grew up in a Pentecostal church. Besides rehearsing for the Christmas program, few things that happened on Christmas Sunday were pre-planned. In contrast with many Advent celebrations, prayers weren't practiced and sermons weren't scripted. Despite those realities, I recently recognized that the Advent themes of hope, peace, joy, and love—though not followed in the formal fashion—were indeed present in my former church's Christmas celebrations each time church members reprised their roles in the Nativity play or choir members sang their soulful songs.

I'm not sure what other churches I'll attend in my lifetime or whether those churches will observe Advent. Neither matters. As long as I acknowledge Jesus as my true hope, my Prince of Peace, my everlasting love, and my source of inexplicable joy, I will experience the essence of Advent wherever I worship. —ERICKA LOYNES

FAITH STEP: *Reflect on ways you've experienced Jesus and then find a quiet place to worship Him.*

Friday, December 13

The true light that gives light to everyone was coming into the world.
John 1:9 (NIV)

A SINGLE STRING OF WHITE Christmas lights lines the windowsills of my sunroom office. It's the one strand of lights that doesn't need to be pulled from the bins of Christmas decorations every December. They stay in place all year. On any given evening, I'll plug in those lights to remind myself and anyone passing that light lives here. The Light of the World.

Today's news report was hard to hear. And a friend was diagnosed with not one but three major health concerns. Another friend's grave disappointment weighs on my heart. And someone I care about is facing a long and complicated recovery. I plugged in my lights to illuminate the growing darkness of my heart heaviness. They remind me of a costly and beautiful answer to encroaching darkness. Jesus, the Light of the World.

While trying to relatch a sunroom window the other day, I accidentally stepped on one of the bulbs in that string. It crunched like a potato chip underfoot. I thought that might be the end of my windowsill reminder until I could replace the set. But they'd been wired so one broken bulb didn't affect the others. They're still shining as brightly as ever.

One diagnosis (or three) can't snuff the light that Jesus offers. One disappointment (or a thousand) won't dim the light of His presence. Bad news can't overwhelm the light that Jesus gives. I'm clinging to that powerful Light. —CYNTHIA RUCHTI

FAITH STEP: *Even if you haven't decorated for Christmas yet, consider putting up one string of lights somewhere to remind you that Jesus is the Light of the World.*

SATURDAY, DECEMBER 14

Do not fear, for I am with you.... Isaiah 41:10 (NIV)

THE FIRST CHRISTMAS AFTER MY divorce, I was devastated. I couldn't imagine what it would be like to celebrate the holiday now that divorce shattered the "perfect Christian family" image I'd worked so hard to cultivate. Past holidays of Christmas cards with family pictures in matching velvet and bows, a miniature lighted Christmas village along the kitchen bar, mistletoe over the doorways, tiny twinkling trees in every room of the house bearing themed ornaments, brightly wrapped presents, and the pièce de résistance, our nine-feet Christmas tree in the living room with our children's handmade ornaments, now seemed to mock me.

The logistics of getting everything down from the attic, unpacking, and setting up all those decorations during a health crisis as my divorce was being finalized was too much. I managed to do what I could. I doubted it was enough.

After exchanging gifts with my kids on Christmas morning, gratitude like I'd not felt in a while bubbled up. No, the house wasn't elaborately decorated and my marriage was ending, but as we sat together in front of the fireplace, I felt content. I realized my efforts would never be enough, but Jesus, Immanuel, was. Immanuel, God with us. God with us outshines any family image I strived to create. The perfect gift of heaven, with me in my imperfection and pain. God with us is the promise of Christmas. And it is more than enough. —GWEN FORD FAULKENBERRY

FAITH STEP: *Sit quietly for a moment and look around your house. Thank Jesus for being with you. He is enough, no matter your circumstances.*

SATURDAY, DECEMBER 14

So Joseph also went up from the town of Nazareth in Galilee to Judea, to Bethlehem the town of David, because he belonged to the house and line of David. He went there to register with Mary, who was pledged to be married to him and was expecting a child. Luke 2:4–5 *(NIV)*

WHEN MY TWO OLDEST BOYS were young, they were invited to be extras in our church Christmas pageant. Their job was to blend into the crowd, reminding the audience of the families that had to travel to Bethlehem for the census. They embraced their roles as first-century travelers, but they got more and more restless during the long performances. Canaan found a rubber fish in the prop room and convinced me to let him take it with him onstage. He called it Bob the Fish, and I'll never forget the moment the cameras zoomed in on him just as he got his brother's attention and began opening and closing Bob's mouth, dancing the fish around as if it were singing an Elvis-style solo.

At first I was mortified and couldn't believe the cameraman had focused on my child just as he was misbehaving. But then I realized that was what real life was like when Jesus was born. I imagined Bethlehem, alive with activity, and wondered if Mary or Joseph ever poked their head out of the stable to hush the children as they raced by because their newborn was finally sleeping. Jesus, the Prince of Peace, was born in the middle of real life, chaos and all. —EMILY E. RYAN

FAITH STEP: *Experience the peace of Jesus by going to a crowded place and reading the story of Christmas in the middle of the noise and activity.*

SATURDAY, DECEMBER 14

He says, "Be still, and know that I am God; I will be exalted among the nations, I will be exalted in the earth." Psalm 46:10 (NIV)

HANGING IN MY LIVING ROOM is a picture frame with the words: "Make time for the quiet moments as God whispers and the world is loud." I purchased it years ago after an unusually hectic Christmas season. Lost in the hustle and bustle, there were only a few short days before December 25, and I struggled to find time for Jesus. My calendar was consumed with celebrations, carol singing, and feasting. However, the peacefulness of the season is where my heart truly rejoices, and that year I felt lost.

Turning out the light of my living room after yet another party, I was exhausted. The only light shining was coming from the tiny bulbs of our Christmas tree. My eyes wandered to our Nativity nestled underneath the glowing branches. I closed my eyes, imagining myself in the fields with the shepherds that night long ago. The hush from Bethlehem falling over their fields. The only sound from the bleating sheep. The star their only light, as a new day dawned for all mankind. The praise and glorification of the angels drawing them into the celebration of Jesus's birth. With all of them, I knelt before my little crèche soaking in His peace and my heart filled with joy in anticipation of His birth. No longer did I feel lost. Jesus found me.

—GLORIA JOYCE

FAITH STEP: *Take a quiet moment to read Luke 2 tonight. Picture yourself witnessing Jesus's birth and quietly praise Him for His gift to you and to all mankind.*

JOY

God of Joy, let all who take refuge in
You be glad; let them ever sing for joy.
Grant that as Jesus promised, His joy may
be in us and our joy may be complete.

Help us learn that, though we may grieve,
our grief will turn to joy. Teach us to always
pray with joy. Grant us such love and
faith that we may always be filled with an
inexpressible and glorious joy. Amen.

Third Sunday of Advent, December 15

*He will be a joy and delight to you, and many will rejoice
because of his birth. Luke 1:14 (NIV)*

I LOVE THAT MOMENT RIGHT before a movie starts, or a vacation begins, or a bride takes her first step down the aisle. That moment of anticipation is full of great promise: magic is about to begin, the possibilities are endless, and hope is at its peak. For me, that anticipation brings almost as much joy as the event itself. That is Advent.

Advent is the drumroll before the grand announcement, the cliffhanger before the commercial break, and the heartbeat right before the miracle. Something wonderful is about to happen, the greatest Something that has ever been. We're meant to savor this time, let it fill us with all that wonder and delight.

Most delightful of all is that when Christmas does come, it arrives in the form of God wrapped in the flesh of His infant Son. And what brings more hope and promise than a baby?

As I walk through this Advent season, I want to keep my hands and heart open, ready and waiting to receive the Christ Child. Just the thought of cradling the Savior of the world in my arms causes a deep joy to bubble up from within, like the rising of the curtain on the stage of the main event—His coming birth. —CLAIRE MCGARRY

FAITH STEP: *Empty your hands and fold your arms as if you were cradling a baby. Feel the joy as you meditate on receiving the Savior of the world when He comes on Christmas morn.*

THIRD SUNDAY OF ADVENT, DECEMBER 15

See! I am coming soon. Revelation 22:12 (NLV)

I WAS DREAMING OF CELEBRATING a leisurely, Jesus-honoring Christmas at home. Don't we all? Our 29-year-old married daughter, Monique, and her family, who'd lived out-of-state for three years, joined us in Portland that year. With our three grown children and three young grandkids all together, I anticipated a relaxed, happy day.

Christmas afternoon arrived. While bustling around getting dinner ready, our daughter Celine asked, "When are we eating?"

"Soon," I answered. The mouthwatering smells wafting through the house made us all hungry. At three o'clock, we sat down to a scrumptious dinner. While cleaning up, someone requested we have dessert. Apparently, the strawberry cheesecake had been calling her name since she saw it in the refrigerator. I hadn't taken more than one bite when one of the kids whined, "When do we open presents?"

"Soon," I answered, trying to rein in my impatience at their impatience. Waiting is hard. For weeks, I'd been eagerly anticipating Christmas by decorating, shopping, wrapping, and cooking, but the truth is that Christmas arrives, and is over, all too soon.

The word *soon* can mean a few minutes, like the time we took to pile dishes in the sink and gather in the front room to read the Christmas story before opening presents. In the case of my last months of pregnancy, my baby couldn't come soon enough. It has been centuries, which is a very long time to me, but Jesus used the word *soon* to refer to His second coming to earth.

No matter who calls me to hurry, today I commit to celebrate a leisurely, Jesus-honoring Advent Sunday because I know Christmas is coming soon. —JENNIFER ANNE F. MESSING

FAITH STEP: *Do one relaxing thing to honor Jesus today—and make it soon!*

THIRD SUNDAY OF ADVENT, DECEMBER 15

Rejoice in the Lord always. I will say it again: Rejoice!
Philippians 4:4 (NIV)

I'M ALWAYS DISAPPOINTED BY WHAT little time I have to enjoy the Christmas season. It's not because the time between the day after Thanksgiving and the weekend after New Year's is short; it's because I'm busy and usually don't get my tree up until December 15. That leaves me with less than half the time most people have to revel in the holiday spirit.

Even though Christmas comes the same day every year, I feel taken by surprise when it's time to put away my decorations. Last Christmas, the room where my family spends the most time together got a much-needed facelift. We rearranged the furniture to give us more open space, and ordered additional strands of Christmas lights, holiday trimmings, wall hangings, and decorative signs to spruce up the place. We couldn't get enough of how the spiraling lights on our tree filled our white walls with a kaleidoscope of glowing rainbow colors. So instead of taking down everything after New Year's, I left it up for months after Christmas for our family to enjoy.

Admittedly, I felt slightly embarrassed by not keeping with the traditional timing of the holiday, especially when I opened the blinds, exposing the fact that it was still Christmas at our house in March. But those decorations and the thoughts they produced kept my family and me joyful long after the holiday was done. And that's nothing to be embarrassed about. —ERICKA LOYNES

FAITH STEP: *After Christmas, take a day or two to spread more holiday cheer. Leave your decorations up, keep your festive lights on, or give a beautifully wrapped gift to a neighbor to continue the spirit of Christmas.*

Monday, December 16

Each of you should give what you have decided in your heart to give, not reluctantly or under compulsion, for God loves a cheerful giver. 2 Corinthians 9:7 (NIV)

As a Girl Scout leader, I thought the Christmas season was the perfect time to teach the troop about the true spirit of giving. When asked what they thought of when they heard the word *Christmas,* these third graders shouted, "Presents!"

"Well, we're working on our Bliss: Live It! Give It! badge," I reminded them. My goal was to teach them the joy of Christmas was so much more exciting when given away to others. I have to admit, the art of giving took a lot of planning and permission slips. I recruited a few of the parents to drive and chaperone. Our first outing was to Walmart. We had enough dues money for each girl to buy a gift for a child in need. I was surprised when they took an hour picking out the perfect presents. They left the store wearing smiles.

Next we drove to an assisted living facility. The girls were nervous about singing Christmas carols in front of the residents. When we entered, no one was in the common area except a friendly greeter. She told us to just start singing. It didn't take long for their timid voices to rise and stir the residents from their rooms. Some elders sang along or clapped their hands.

Looking at the smiles on my Girl Scouts' faces, I knew they would answer my question differently now. I believe presents were the furthest thing from their minds now that they'd experienced the true spirit of giving. —Jeannie Hughes

---

Faith Step: *Think of three ways you can give rather than receive this Christmas.*

MONDAY, DECEMBER 16

The lines have fallen for me in pleasant places; indeed, I have a beautiful inheritance. Psalm 16:6 (ESV)

THUNK! SINCE IT WAS THE Christmas season, I recognized the sound— a package being tossed on the porch by the UPS driver. "You got a package, Honey," my grandson called, not excited in the least.

How times had changed! At Christmastime when I was growing up, my brothers and I waited at the window, listening for the rumble of the mail truck. We didn't get many packages back then, but the one we anticipated most was the box from Duluth, Minnesota, our Norwegian grandmother Nellie's Christmas *krumkaker.* The delicate Norwegian waffle cookies, baked on a hot iron and shaped into a cone, were sometimes broken in transit, but they still tasted heavenly.

My brothers and I never tired of hearing Grandmother's story— how she and Grandfather Hilmar, both in their early twenties, had left Norway on a boat and settled in Minnesota. How Hilmar, a commercial fisherman, drowned on Thanksgiving Day, 1923, trying to save his brother from the icy waters of Lake Superior. How Nellie raised six young children alone, leaning on Jesus, on whom she counted most of all.

As proud as I am of my Norwegian heritage, I'm prouder still of my heritage in Jesus, whose birthday we celebrate. I never tire of hearing of His stories, His kindness, His miraculous healings, His ultimate sacrifice. Because of Jesus, I have a beautiful inheritance. And that's something to be excited about! —PAT BUTLER DYSON

FAITH STEP: *Bake or cook a familiar dish that your grandparent made during your childhood. Tell someone the life story of the recipe's originator.*

MONDAY, DECEMBER 16

But as for me, I watch in hope for the LORD, I wait for God my Savior; my God will hear me. Micah 7:7 (NIV)

FROM MY DESK, I CAN look out the window and see the trees in our front yard. Their tall, gray-brown trunks stretch bare limbs to reach the sun. This winter view is such a picture of the yearning my heart feels to hang on to the spirit of Advent.

Before I know it, spring will appear on the horizon, and Advent will be a view of the past. Yet my heart longs—no, it needs—to keep the spirit of Advent fresh after the candle wreath and other Christmas décor are put away.

Advent invites us to expect Jesus to appear in our midst, as He did on the night of His birth, and in a way no one anticipated. Yet He doesn't want us to pack up that expectation with the Christmas décor and tuck it away for the next 12 months.

I love the yearly rhythm of the calendar, as it rolls toward Advent, then eases away into a fresh set of months. Each time through, it combines unique challenges and opportunities to experience Jesus's presence.

Advent invites me to hold on to its spirit and continue to expect that I will see Jesus in the normal moments every day. I love that reality so much. —ERIN KEELEY MARSHALL

FAITH STEP: *Place a small candle in your desk pen holder or on the kitchen windowsill to remind you to keep the Advent spirit alive. Ask Jesus to help you expect His presence and provision all year.*

TUESDAY, DECEMBER 17

Our mouths were filled with laughter, our tongues with songs of joy.
Then it was said among the nations, "The LORD has done great things for
them." The LORD has done great things for us, and we are filled with joy."
Psalm 126:2–3 *(NIV)*

MY FAMILY AND I ARE not only children of God but kids at heart. We believe in Jesus—and in His sense of humor. Martin Luther said this about laughter: "If I am not allowed to laugh in heaven, I don't want to go there." I wouldn't go that far, but humor is important to me.

On Christmas Eve I fidgeted as my daughter unwrapped the ice cream maker we'd chosen for her and our son-in-law. Would they like it? An unreadable expression flashed across her face for an instant, followed by a grin. I breathed a sigh of relief. My turn came next, and upon opening the package from my husband, I was thrilled. I too had received an ice cream maker. When we unwrapped the present the kids had chosen for David and me, we discovered another ice cream maker. Then Christina and Eric exchanged their gifts with each other. Two more of them. This was absurd. Had we entered another world where people existed solely on icy treats? Four people. Five ice cream makers. We had to laugh, and I suspect Jesus chuckled alongside.

But as I reflect on our Christmas Eve fiasco, I think Jesus also delivered a divine message. When things go sideways—at gift exchanges and in life—it's best to laugh and give thanks. To remember we're not alone. And to smile, knowing God too gives every believer the same perfect gift, His Son, Jesus. —HEIDI GAUL

FAITH STEP: *Jesus is the perfect one-size-fits-all-forever gift. Pray for opportunities and wisdom to share Him this season.*

TUESDAY, DECEMBER 17

---

*Until now you have not asked for anything in my name. Ask and you
will receive, and your joy will be complete. John 16:24 (NIV)*

MY SON ISAAC IS 13. Isaac has Down syndrome, so while he's very
much a typical middle schooler in some ways, in other ways he's
delightfully childlike. Though he's always enjoyed Christmas, last
year he was bursting with joyful interest in all things merry and
bright. I suspect it's due to his growing mature understanding coupled with his little boy's innocence. I have a tendency to get bogged
down with holiday chores, but Isaac's joy is contagious.

He had definite opinions about the gifts he wanted, and because
he still believes in Santa, we had extra fun exploring options and
making wish lists. He's very eager to decorate and loves helping,
taking his responsibilities seriously, especially regarding placing
baby Jesus in the manger. He has two toy Nativities and plays with
them throughout the season.

Isaac loves Christmas music, which we play nonstop in the car,
singing along loudly. We drive through Florida's abundant, festively
lit neighborhoods several times in December. Sweetly imaginative,
Isaac talks about Rudolph and Frosty as though they were real-life
best buddies.

From the moment the season begins, Isaac asks what's next each
step of the way. He inquires about decorating the tree, setting out
the Christmas village, shopping, seeing neighborhood lights, baking cookies, going to parties, attending church activities…the whole
shebang. When the holiday frazzle sets in, Isaac's unbridled joy
makes my joy complete. Thanks, Isaac! —ISABELLA CAMPOLATTARO

FAITH STEP: *If you find yourself frazzled by holiday prep, grab a hot drink and
take a break to enjoy your decorations with the eyes of a child, if not an actual
little one.*

TUESDAY, DECEMBER 17

Every good gift, every perfect gift, comes from above. James 1:17 (CEB)

I LOVE SHOPPING FOR CHRISTMAS gifts. Except when I hate it. I want so badly to choose a present that the recipient will enjoy, something that will make their life easier. I want it to be their favorite color and a perfect fit. Maybe something they've wanted for a long time. With adults, that's often an impossible quest. But with children it's easier to hit the mark. Last fall my grandson was practically drooling over a chess master's upcoming book release. My two younger granddaughters longed for those colorful instant cameras. The teal green was hard to find, but I was all over it.

The time and money I invest in Christmas shopping is nothing compared to the joy I receive as I watch my loved ones unwrap their gifts. My loving Father receives joy in showering me with gifts every day. He's already given me far beyond what I deserve in His gifts of salvation and new life made possible through Jesus.

My adult children usually respond with "I don't know" when I ask for gift ideas. But children know what they want and are not afraid to ask for it, even if it sounds outrageous. I want to be comfortable enough with Jesus to share my heart's desires even when they seem too outrageous to me. I can trust Him to provide the gift, withhold it for my good, or send a substitute that will be even better.
—DIANNE NEAL MATTHEWS

FAITH STEP: *Is there something you've been longing for but have been reluctant to ask for? Trust Jesus enough to talk to Him about it right now.*

WEDNESDAY, DECEMBER 18

When they saw the star, they rejoiced with exceedingly great joy.
Matthew 2:10 (NKJV)

HAVE YOU SEEN VIDEOS (OR been part of one) where a sibling or a new grandparent walks into a birthing center room and is overcome with joy at the sight of the newborn? It's especially heart-tugging to see a toddler tenderly reach for the child, stroke its downy head, sit near Mom, and ask to hold the baby. It's like emotional fireworks and grateful tears when a grandparent sees a new grandchild for the first time, more fully aware than the sibling that they're looking at a miracle. What a happy scene! So much joy. But possibly subdued in some ways by the presence of a healing mother and a sleeping babe.

I'm contrasting that obvious but intentionally controlled joy with what the magi experienced when they stood on the threshold of seeing Jesus. "Exceedingly great joy." It's the kind of phrase English teachers might direct students to trim. "Do you need an adverb, an adjective, and a strong verb to say this?"

The joy of the magi was so profound, one word couldn't describe it on its own. The star they'd been following had stopped moving. It shone brightly over the place where Jesus and family were staying. A star stopped. "He's here," it silently communicated. They were so overwhelmed, it took an excess of words to describe their excessive joy.

Is that my heart's attitude as I stand on the threshold of "seeing" Christ anew this Christmas? —CYNTHIA RUCHTI

FAITH STEP: *Create a list of words to capture your joy this Advent season. Share them with Jesus when you talk to Him today.*

WEDNESDAY, DECEMBER 18

When Elizabeth heard Mary's greeting, the baby leaped in her womb, and Elizabeth was filled with the Holy Spirit. In a loud voice she exclaimed: "Blessed are you among women, and blessed is the child you will bear!"
Luke 1:41–42 (NIV)

MY MOM LIVES ABOUT 35 minutes away. That's not far in driving terms, but when you have three kids involved in multiple activities, it makes it far more challenging to get down to her house and back before the next commitment begins. Needless to say, we don't get there as often as we should.

Making it a priority last week, we drove down to her house to help her decorate for Christmas. When we arrived, she greeted us at the door with a radiant smile, gratitude on her lips, and fervent hugs all around. She rolled out the red carpet of snacks and dinner, treating us as if we were royalty! She was so filled with exuberant joy at our visit, it reminded me of Elizabeth greeting the mother of Jesus when Mary went to visit. Without a doubt, my mom made us feel blessed among people. And when our visit ended, she stood at the front door and waved as we pulled away, extending yet another blessing for our journey home.

It occurred to me as I headed home that I could follow her example and welcome others with the same joy she showed my family. Doing so might awaken the Christ Child within each of us so we feel His gentle leap in our hearts, reminding us that we are all sacred vessels carrying Christmas within. —CLAIRE MCGARRY

FAITH STEP: *Choose one person to visit this week and greet them with such joy that they feel special and blessed.*

WEDNESDAY, DECEMBER 18

The way a rainbow springs out of the sky on a rainy day—that's what it was like. It turned out to be the Glory of GOD! Ezekiel 1:28 (MSG)

ONE OF THE FACETS I love most about Christmas is the vast display of colors. Strings of jewel-toned lights on houses and trees. Sparkly dresses. Glittering shoes. And one of my favorites: seeing brightly wrapped presents through car windows.

One year when our kids were still kids, we decided to brave the two-day drive from our home in Los Angeles to Portland, Oregon, to visit Kevin's family. After singing every Christmas carol we knew, we entertained ourselves by spotting gifts piled in vehicles.

"Oh, look at that VW van! There must be presents in a hundred colors in their back window!" We overlooked the slight exaggeration on Ron's part, and made up stories about what surprises those packages held.

"Ooooh, that car next to us has lots of purple wrapping paper!" Kevin and I exchanged grins at Esther's love of all things purple. As I thought about the colors of Christmas, I realized they told the story of Jesus. White for the star that filled the night sky with a blinding blaze to guide the shepherds to Jesus's birthplace. Red represents the blood of Jesus poured out on Calvary's cross, to cleanse us of every sin. Deep emerald, the shade of evergreen trees, symbolizes our new life in Jesus. Gold, of course, signifies the gifts the magi brought to the Christ child.

But the colors I see on Christmas presents through car windows can't compare to the real gift, Jesus Himself. —JEANETTE LEVELLIE

FAITH STEP: *As you wrap packages, be aware of your color choices. Which color of Christmas is the most meaningful for you?*

THURSDAY, DECEMBER 19

But the angel said to them, "Do not be afraid. I bring you good news that will cause great joy for all the people." Luke 2:10 (NIV)

EVER SINCE I WAS A child, Christmas has been my favorite holiday. Back then joy came as easy as picking out what I wanted from the big Sears catalog, knowing Santa would bring at least some of it. We weren't wealthy but my parents were hard-working teachers with steady jobs. Home had a warm fireplace. Daddy put up the tree. Moma hung stands of bubble lights on the boughs. My brother and I decorated the branches with heirloom ornaments. Granny and PaPa joined us for Christmas dinner.

Now that I am older, I understand that those were "the good old days" and my circumstances were ideal for a child. I'm sure there were adult stresses from which my parents shielded me, but life seemed simple, joyful, and good.

As an adult, life is more complicated. I've learned that joy is more a choice of my will than a product of my circumstances. But what is Christmas if not the declaration that joy came to the world through difficult circumstances? An unwed, teenage mother delivering her baby to an audience of animals, in manure and hay, as an outsider who was far from home. And yet the angel saw joy born in these circumstances and proclaimed tidings of great joy for all people.

When I meditate on the glorious gift of His birth, my life again seems simple, joyful, and good. —GWEN FORD FAULKENBERRY

FAITH STEP: *Sing a few carols of joy and renew your strength as you meditate on Jesus's birth. Suggestions: "Joy to the World," "God Rest Ye Merry, Gentlemen," "Hark! The Herald Angels Sing"*

THURSDAY, DECEMBER 19

"I am the Lord's servant," Mary answered. "May your word to me be fulfilled." Then the angel left her. Luke 1:38 *(NIV)*

ONE OF MY FAVORITE CHRISTMASTIME decorations is my white porcelain Nativity. Every year we set it up with great care and place the baby Jesus front and center, just as He is in our lives. But this year, I find myself fascinated with young Mary, positioned beside His cradle, a look of reverence on her small face. The real Mary was so young—only a teenager—when she was told of her fateful future. And yet she answered the angel that relayed God's message without hesitancy. She faced an unwed pregnancy with acceptance and gave birth in a far-off town with no one but her husband Joseph to help her during labor. And she held to her dignity through it all.

Sermons often ask the question, "Why did God find favor in Mary?" I think the answer lies in her inherent personality traits: love and respect for God, humility, patience, tenacity, obedience, and a hidden strength we can only begin to understand. Those very aspects of her spirit joined with God's utter perfection in the creation of Jesus.

Setting my porcelain Mary back in her spot beside our Lord, I wonder, As I strive to be more like Jesus, could He be smiling down, seeing a bit of Mary in me? I smile. I hope so. —HEIDI GAUL

FAITH STEP: *List the traits you admire most in Mary. Endeavor to make those traits your own as you move through Advent.*

THURSDAY, DECEMBER 19

You see that his faith and his actions were working together, and his faith was made complete by what he did. James 2:22 (NIV)

WHEN I WAS GROWING UP in the 1960s in West Virginia, Christmas was a busy season in our home. Not only was it a time to decorate, but my siblings and I crowded at the kitchen counter to help/watch our mother with candy making. The sweet aromas of milk chocolate, peanut butter, and caramel filled the air. I can almost taste it, even today.

With one brother and sister, we children helped when we could. But mostly the coconut bon-bons, caramel pecan turtles, and peanut butter–dipped buckeyes were made by our mother's hands. I don't know how she had the energy to create such wonderful confections. It took several days.

After the candy was finished, we kids placed a sample of each variety on a Christmas-themed paper plate. With the candies covered with plastic wrap and topped with a bow, we set out for our first deliveries of the home-made gifts to our neighbors. Our hands were cold from the frosty weather, but our hearts were always full from our actions.

I loved sharing our delicious candy with friends, family, and neighbors. This tradition taught me at an early age that Christmas was about giving. —JEANNIE HUGHES

FAITH STEP: *Think of one way you might share the gift of giving during Christmas. It doesn't have to be a grand gesture, just a simple act will do.*

FRIDAY, DECEMBER 20

You make known to me the path of life; you will fill me with joy in your presence, with eternal pleasures at your right hand. Psalm 16:11 (NIV)

AT THE CRACK OF DAWN on Christmas morning, our adult children and their families arrive at our house and enter via the kitchen door to the smell of bacon sizzling on the griddle, waffles cooking on the iron, and fresh coffee brewing. It's not that the breakfast itself is anything special. They could just as easily eat at their own homes, but I think it's the excitement and joy of once again being together—back at Mom and Dad's house—that carries this holiday ritual.

There are hugs all around as, one after another, they arrive. There's a sweet sharing of recent stories as we sit down to eat together. There's a thrill of anticipation as we wipe the last drop of syrup from our mouths and make our way to the living room to exchange gifts. There's an atmosphere of harmony, love, and fun as we take the time to watch each other open packages and dump out our stockings. I relish this morning tradition. Being in the presence of my family reminds me how much Jesus enjoys the presence of my company, His beloved daughter. —KRISTEN WEST

FAITH STEP: *Make a meal with the intention of being in Jesus's presence. As you sit down at the table, be fully present for Him.*

FRIDAY, DECEMBER 20

Taste and see that the LORD is good; blessed is the one who takes refuge in him.
Psalm 34:8 *(NIV)*

ANYONE WHO KNOWS ME KNOWS that I love most chocolatey things. I was hooked as a kid at those after-church bake sales where a piece of double-layered chocolate cake the size of my head cost only a dollar. Whenever I was given permission to buy one, I was ecstatic!

Often, without my asking, my husband brings me a couple of Snickers bars from a quick trip to the grocery store or gas station. When I see those shiny brown plastic-wrapped chocolate bars on the table, I am thrilled and filled with joy. At the earliest possible moment, I take a bite. The tasty indulgence is a scrumptious moment of goodness no matter what's going on around me.

Unlike a delicious candy bar, life is not always sweet and satisfying. It's often soured by bitter realities that can be hard to swallow: caring for aging parents, grieving the loss of a loved one, and lamenting a world that can be simultaneously beautiful and punishing. Yet Jesus is good. Always. No matter what external conditions are closing in on me, I can partake of the inexplicable lasting goodness of Jesus. —ERICKA LOYNES

FAITH STEP: *Grab your favorite treat in one hand and your Bible in the other. Find as many scriptures as you can about the goodness of Jesus and meditate on them.*

Friday, December 20

I praise you for remembering me in everything and for holding to the traditions just as I passed them on to you. 1 Corinthians 11:2 *(NIV)*

GAZING AT OUR DECORATED CHRISTMAS tree, I smiled at the unique ornaments hanging there. It seemed like only yesterday when our tree was filled with simple colored balls. Now our tree tells the story of our family, one ornament at a time. It was a tradition my husband, Matt, and I began when we married a quarter of a century ago. When we took a trip, we purchased an ornament as our souvenir. Adding the new ornament to our tree at Christmas, we removed a colored ball. Taking the ornaments out and unwrapping them each year, we recounted the stories with our children bringing them into the precious history of our love. Friends and family who visit our home ask about the year's new ornament. Others may notice something different about an older one. We happily share the stories again and again.

Like our tree, the Bible is filled with the precious history of Jesus and His love story with us. From the beginnings of the world in Genesis until His death on the Cross, Jesus shows His love for us. Opening our Bible, we unwrap His stories and delight at each retelling of Jesus's love and sacrifice. Many times, we read the familiar stories with excitement, recalling the first time we heard it. Other times, we see His life with new eyes. Yet in every retelling, they become more familiar and beautiful. We happily read these stories again and again. —GLORIA JOYCE

FAITH STEP: *Open your Bible and ask Jesus to surprise you with a retelling of one of His precious stories.*

SATURDAY, DECEMBER 21

These things I have spoken to you, that My joy may remain in you,
and that your joy may be full. John 15:11 (NKJV)

DIGGING THROUGH A BOX OF old Christmas photos, I came across a treasured picture from my childhood: a ragtag gang of kids singing carols, led by a grinning girl in a baseball cap—Bonnie. We must have been singing "Joy to the World," because that was Bonnie's favorite.

From birth, Bonnie had experienced multiple challenges, but they didn't dim her joy. She was a free-range kid like the rest of us, riding bikes, playing games, or catching fish at the pond. Bonnie's dad modified her bike to help her ride. She couldn't run fast, but she could kick, and she was an enthusiastic cheerleader for her team. At the pond, she was an ace with a cane pole.

Nobody locked their doors in our neighborhood, and Bonnie was a frequent visitor to all our homes. Sometimes she'd drop in for supper or play with our cats till we finished eating. She relished being the reporter of news—passing on tidbits about the Cains' new baby, Grandma Gray's fender-bender, the Lindners' missing collie. Surely Jesus was her sidekick as she roamed the neighborhood, spreading goodwill wherever she went. Bonnie loved everyone and everyone loved her.

Most of all, Bonnie liked to sing. Her face shone with the love of Jesus when she sang, whether in the choir at the First Baptist Church or Christmas carols in the neighborhood. Just by being herself, Bonnie taught me a valuable lesson about finding joy, no matter the circumstances. —PAT BUTLER DYSON

FAITH STEP: *Think of the most consistently joyful person you know. Ask them for tips on how they do it.*

SATURDAY, DECEMBER 21

Many ask favors of a generous person — to a giver of gifts,
everyone is a friend. Proverbs 19:6 (CJB)

OKAY, I CONFESS. I LOVE presents.

Not only getting them but also giving. Especially giving. Some of my happiest moments are spent shopping for others. I can always remember what everyone's favorite color is, whether they like dark or milk chocolate, and if they prefer cats, dogs, or guinea pigs.

I get over-the-moon excited when my husband, Kevin, unwraps a present I know he'll love. A vintage record from a Southern gospel singing group. His favorite, nearly-impossible-to-find candies. Or an antique book volume he's looked for in every used bookstore from Pittsburgh to Portland. I've even been known to clap my hands, jump up and down, and sing like an opera star on steroids when Kev opens a treasure I found for him.

It makes me wonder how God felt as He sent Jesus to earth that starry night in Bethlehem. When Mary cuddled God's Beloved in her arms for the first time, did God clap and spin in circles and laugh until tears ran down His face? Did He sing loud and dance hard and turn the stars into fireworks?

Our love of giving surely comes from the extravagant heart of God. From that first couple in the garden to Mary and Joseph to every individual now, God knew what we needed and wanted most. Something that would fit perfectly and bring tears of gratitude to our eyes. Something we weren't even aware that we needed until He arrived. A Savior. A King. A Friend.

Jesus is that gift. —JEANETTE LEVELLIE

FAITH STEP: *Thank God for sending His perfect gift, Jesus.*

SATURDAY, DECEMBER 21

The shepherds said to one another, "Let's go to Bethlehem and see this thing that has happened, which the Lord has told us about." Luke 2:15 (NIV)

MY FAMILY HAS TWO FURRY members we love. Bea and Boone are Bichon Frisé and miniature poodle mixes who appear to greet each day with anticipation that is infectious.

Bea is reserved, gentle, and loving. She wakes early and brings an even-keeled, mild approach to life, like an old soul who thinks deep thoughts. Boone is our family's lone extrovert. He brings full-throttle energy into his day until he crashes at night, not to be heard from again until late the following morning.

They illustrate that anticipation is unique. It's full-hearted and oozes from them, prompting me to follow their lead.

Watching them, I consider how my anticipation shows as I prepare to celebrate Jesus's birth.

Some days, pondering the gift of Jesus's life quiets me with deep gratitude. Other moments, thoughts of His birth thrill me because of all it means.

How about you? Does the gift of His birth prompt a smile or even laughter at the wonder?

This Advent season, will you thoughtfully anticipate Jesus's birthday? Your circumstances and frame of mind this year are unique to any other time. Your anticipation will be unique because this exact Advent season will happen only once.

When I put my heart into anticipating Jesus's birthday, I hope my anticipation will spread infectiously to others. After all, the world still rejoices with the shepherds' anticipation 2,000 years later.

—ERIN KEELEY MARSHALL

FAITH STEP: *What words express your Advent anticipation? Write them down and meditate on your list throughout the day.*

LOVE

God of Love, You demonstrated Your love
for us in this: While we were still sinners,
Christ died for us. I trust in Your unfailing
love. Teach me to love You with all my heart,
soul, mind, and strength.

Teach me to love my neighbor, to love
my enemies, and to do good to all. Help
me to remain in Your love. Help me to
do everything in love, as I live by faith in
the Son of God, who loved me and gave
Himself for me. Amen.

Fourth Sunday of Advent, December 22

"'Love the Lord your God with all your heart and with all your soul and with all your mind and with all your strength.' The second is this: 'Love your neighbor as yourself.' There is no commandment greater than these."
Mark 12:30–31 (NIV)

The handmade gift my sister spent hours on, making sure it was just right. The hug from my husband Christmas morning. The stack of cards on the coffee table, sent from friends all over the map. Phone calls with out-of-state family. The tenderness in my daughter and son-in-law's eyes when they speak of each other to me.

It's love. Every bit of it, spread thick as frosting on cake throughout this season. Unlike some of the presents I shop for, this exchange of affection is authentic, free, and best when returned. I see it reflected in the faces of neighbors and shopkeepers, children and seniors alike.

More than the warm fuzzy feelings we might delight in at Christmas, devotion to God should be powerful, including every aspect of our being: heart, soul, mind, and strength. And the affection we offer others should mirror our own self-love. In John 13:34, Jesus says to love one another as He has loved us. This love needs to be as deep, selfless, and universal as that which Jesus lavishes on believers.

Jesus's commands are simple and straightforward. Love God and everyone we meet, even the unlovable. Love ourselves. We love because He first loved us (1 John 4:19, NIV). And through this love we are made whole. —Heidi Gaul

Faith Step: *Make a list of those dear to you. Think of ways—free of cost—that you can shower them with love during this season.*

Fourth Sunday of Advent, December 22

And so we know and rely on the love God has for us. God is love. Whoever lives in love lives in God, and God in them. 1 John 4:16 (NIV)

A FEW YEARS AGO, I was hosting a table at our church's annual holiday celebration for women. Toward the end of the meal, another staff wife walked up to my table and invited a few of the women to take a picture with her. Just before the camera clicked, she said, "Smile! Pastors' wives club!" At that moment I realized the women she'd chosen for the photo were the wives of ministers, just like me, but she didn't choose me. I'd like to think that her decision to exclude me from the "pastors' wives club" wasn't intentional, but it sure felt like a snub. Instead of feeling happy and excited to celebrate the birth of Jesus with other church women, I felt alone, rejected, and unloved.

On one hand, it doesn't make sense to feel lonely or unloved during Advent. How could we when the entire season is a celebration of God's love for us through the gift of Jesus! But the truth is that many people spend the entire season feeling left out of the party, just like I did at the women's event. I let that moment remind me that the love of Christ is for everyone—even pastors' wives who are left out of pictures—and that I want to be intentional about helping others feel His love during Christmas. —EMILY E. RYAN

FAITH STEP: *Show the love of Christ through invitations. Invite others to join you at church, to visit your home, to sit at your table, and to be in pictures with you.*

Fourth Sunday of Advent, December 22

The light shines in the darkness, and the darkness has not overcome it. John 1:5 (NIV)

In Arkansas we have all four seasons, and I like that. It's always a great relief when our blazing hot, humid summers give way to autumn, which is the loveliest season to me. Across the river from my house are mountains that burst out in vibrant hues along about October. They look like that big box of crayons I used to covet in elementary school, the one with every imaginable color and the sharpener on the side.

I start to get wistful when the leaves fall. Even though winter has its own stark beauty—the bare bones of the trees, bald eagles, and faithful evergreens—it is the darkness that saddens me. The worst is when we "fall back" into not-daylight-saving time and the sunset starts happening around 5 p.m. It encroaches ever closer, it seems, until the winter solstice on December 21, the darkest day of the year.

I know we don't really know the actual date Jesus was born, but I can't help feeling there is poetic justice in the timing of Advent. Celebrating the birth of our Savior—the Light of the World—just as that darkest night ends and the daylight begins to grow is fitting on this fourth Sunday of Advent. Jesus is our hope. His birth made a way for spiritual light to grow in our darkest places. And His Light overcomes the darkness of every season. —Gwen Ford Faulkenberry

---

Faith Step: *Light a candle and let it remind you that Christmas and brighter days are coming.*

MONDAY, DECEMBER 23

But God demonstrates his own love for us in this: While we were still sinners, Christ died for us. Romans 5:8 (NIV)

WHERE'S THE WORD *LOVE* IN Christmas? While working on a talk for a Christmas tea for women, I hoped to find Christmas hymn titles the attendees could mix and match to create their own encouraging Christmas phrases. I found many with *joy, holy, faithful, silent, still, manger, shepherds, angels, adore....*

Love is the whole point of Christmas—God's extravagant love for us in sending His Son. That love is threaded throughout the entire biblical telling of the event we call the first Christmas. A young woman's love for Yahweh led to her surrender to His unique and startling call on her life. A betrothed husband's love for his Lord and Mary compelled him to respond to instructions of God's messenger. The shepherds' reaction to love-filled light that flooded their crude existence with angels who sent the baby announcement first to them. The young mom's tenderness toward the newborn she swaddled as much from heavenly instruction as from tradition.

Love came down at Christmas. The song and the concept. Love may not be in the title of many popular Christmas hymns, but Jesus is the ultimate expression of God's love. And that love tells the whole story. —CYNTHIA RUCHTI

FAITH STEP: *Take a few minutes and listen to your favorite Christmas hymn. Can you hear the love of God, even if the lyrics don't mention the word?*

MONDAY, DECEMBER 23

This is how God showed his love among us: He sent his one and only Son into the world that we might live through him. 1 John 4:9 *(NIV)*

GROWING UP IN THE PHILIPPINES, I loved one of my family's holiday traditions. Each year, my mother invited a group of Christian Christmas carolers to serenade us in our home. They mostly came from humble backgrounds, and everyone in the group—the singers, two guitarists, and two tambourine players—was blind. They entertained for about 30 minutes before enjoying refreshments with us. I truly felt the joy and love they expressed in their vocal performance.

Some of the carolers were accompanied by a spouse, who *could* see. The spouse would help them find a seat or get refreshments. The fellowship time afterwards was always interesting—chatting and learning about their lives. From their cheerful countenances, I often forgot they didn't have sight! Yet I somehow knew that Jesus's love in their hearts had given them eyes to truly see.

Come to think of it, before I accepted Jesus into my heart as a teen, I too could not see. Christ gave me eyes to see with compassion, and the ability to love others with His love. My eye-opening experience with Jesus led me to a holiday tradition of my own—singing His praise as I shower family, friends, and strangers with Jesus's unconditional love. —JENNIFER ANNE F. MESSING

FAITH STEP: *Close your eyes and sing a favorite Christmas carol. Then pray that Jesus shows you how to share His love with someone today.*

MONDAY, DECEMBER 23

Dear friends, let us love one another, for love comes from God. Everyone who loves has been born of God and knows God. 1 John 4:7 (NIV)

WHEN I STARTED EXPLORING MY faith in my thirties, one of my earliest stumbling blocks was wondering why an all-powerful God would sacrifice His only Son to save the human race (John 3:16). I distinctly remember thinking this sacrifice was weird, abstract, impossible to understand, and difficult to accept as truth for a time. Given to inquiry and deep thinking, I contemplated this matter and asked God about it. At the time, I was a childless, unmarried woman with limited exposure to kids or even healthy parents.

I eventually learned that God loved humanity enough to subject Himself and His eternal Son to the fragility of a disadvantaged infancy in a hard environment, the mundane frustrations of human life, relentless persecution and injustice, and finally a cruel and wrongful death. *But why?*

Today, I ask fewer questions of God, and neither need, nor expect, answers. Yet God graciously provided me with a revelation. As a mom of two boys whom I adore above all, I would sacrifice anything for them for one simple reason—because I love them. And that's why God gave this sacrificial gift of Jesus, His only Son, to the world—it was to give His love to us. To me.

Finally, I understood. God did it all for love. —ISABELLA CAMPOLATTARO

FAITH STEP: *What sacrificial action of love can you do to honor God's indescribable gift of Jesus?*

TUESDAY, DECEMBER 24

Thank God for his Son—his Gift too wonderful for words.
2 *Corinthians 9:15 (TLB)*

CHRISTMAS EVE, AND I WAS as excited as a kid! My husband, Jeff, would be home at lunch to try on the new Santa suit I'd bought him to wear for tonight's family celebration at our daughter's house. I smiled, imagining the wonder and delight in my grandchildren's eyes when they saw Santa Claus. My reverie was shattered when Jeff staggered in the door, looking green around the gills. "I'm sick, Pat," he groaned.

"You can't be sick! You have to be Santa!" I wailed. I settled him on the couch with a comforter and brought him a cup of ginger tea and some Tylenol. "You can do this!" I assured him. "What is Christmas without Santa?"

"But what if I expose everyone to what I have?" Jeff said. "Several people at work have the flu." I took his temperature and when the thermometer registered 101 degrees, I reluctantly abandoned my attempts to resuscitate Saint Nick.

Gathering up gifts to take to my daughter's, I couldn't help feeling I'd forgotten someone. *Psst, Pat.* His gentle whisper hit me like a lump of coal. I *had* forgotten Someone, the greatest Gift of them all. *Oh, Jesus, forgive me.* My eyes fell on the Bible in front of our manger scene, open to the second chapter of Luke. Then and there, I sat down by the fire and read the sweetest story ever written. After all, what is Christmas without Jesus? —PAT BUTLER DYSON

FAITH STEP: *Write a thank-you note to God for His miraculous gift of Jesus. Hang the note front and center on the Christmas tree.*

Tuesday, December 24

*The shepherds returned, glorifying and praising God for
all the things they had heard and seen. Luke 2:20 (NIV)*

The shopping is done. The cookies are baked. Festive Christmas
lights illuminate our yard. As excited as I am to be surrounded by
my children, their spouses, and my grandson this evening, I am
equally excited to be at church. Few services hold the sacred weight
and joy that this one does for me. It's here, in the Christmas Eve
service, that I pause and think about the young mother who fully
surrendered herself to bring the Savior into the world. It's here, as I
read through those special passages in Luke 2, that I remember the
arduous journey that Joseph and Mary took, the fear and scrutiny
they must have faced, and the utter dependence on God they exhib-
ited. It's during this special Christmas Eve service that I light and
hold a candle as I sing "O Holy Night" and reflect on that solemn
and historical event centuries ago when a manger held the most
significant child to ever be born. And it's here, in this memorable
service, that I quiet myself and consider God's ultimate act of love
in sending His only begotten Son into the world to save us, knowing
the outcome and, ultimately, what Jesus would eventually have to
endure in order to redeem us from sin.

Like the shepherds centuries ago, I sit in awe glorifying and praising God for what I hear and see as I receive the majesty of God's
perfect gift to the world. —Kristen West

Faith Step: *Is there a special service God might be leading you to attend
(in person or online) this Christmas Eve?*

TUESDAY, DECEMBER 24

---

*For God so loved the world that He gave His only begotten Son,
that whoever believes in Him should not perish but have
everlasting life. John 3:16 (NKJV)*

ONE OF MY HUSBAND'S FAVORITE hobbies is papercraft. David's collection of inks, scissors, stamps, and embossing powders is huge. Every Christmas season he buries the table in supplies, transforming ordinary brown craft paper into unique gift wrap. Only the presents that he deems worthy get this special treatment. When Christmas Eve arrives, we are delighted with gifts depicting any number of other colorful pictures he's dreamed up. The wrap is cherished by family members, almost like a gift encasing another present. David's legacy.

The holiday season reminds me of my husband's labor of love. The care we take, wrapping each other in love and gratitude. The joy shared as we bake cookies, set up the Nativity, and take part in the wonders of the Advent season. Yet all these traditions are only a beautiful wrapper for the real treasure encompassed by the season. The birth of Baby Jesus. Our eternal and glorious gift. He's all we'll ever truly need.

No matter how we spend this evening and Christmas Day, we'll remember the sweet baby who holds our future in His tiny hands, as we reach out to welcome Him into our hearts. Our perfect gift. Jesus. —HEIDI GAUL

FAITH STEP: *Tonight, when life has quieted down, take a few minutes to thank God for His one perfect gift, Jesus.*

WEDNESDAY, DECEMBER 25

"This will be a sign to you: You will find a baby wrapped in cloths and lying in a manger." Suddenly a great company of the heavenly host appeared with the angel, praising God. Luke 2:12–13 (NIV)

MERRY CHRISTMAS! I AIM TO soak up its familiar aura of humble majesty. For me, that pairing of humility and majesty resonates in every moment of this day and embodies who Jesus is.

As I head downstairs to make coffee, the morning holds a humble hush, yet the awakening sky already hints at the day's majesty. Coffee mug in hand, I move to the living room and see the Nativity, that timeless scene of Jesus's humble entrance to earth. Then across the room, I press a button and the tree lights up radiantly. These symbols of the holiday blend the mellow and brilliant, gentle and bold, simple and awesome—humble humanity and majestic holiness. I love that Jesus is fully both. He holds the world together and watches from on high, and He also surrounds my life and shelters my heart.

Christmas is more His day than mine. Born in a humble manger to earthly parents without remarkable resumes, Jesus was visited by shepherds and kings. He lived a supremely common, thoroughly uncommon life. Humble majesty, the perfect oxymoron to describe the Baby, King, and my best friend, Jesus. Happy birthday, Jesus! —ERIN KEELEY MARSHALL

FAITH STEP: *Spend a few moments pondering the phrase* humble majesty. *Then softly sing "Happy Birthday" to Jesus.*

WEDNESDAY, DECEMBER 25

"Though your sins are like scarlet, they shall be as white as snow."
Isaiah 1:18 (NIV)

SNOW ON CHRISTMAS DAY? A sparkling wonder! Despite its beauty, though, the weight of snow can collapse roofs, topple trees, and strand travelers. Beauty and heartache—both. New snow fell overnight and the apple tree outside my office window is bowed low. *And you're just standing there taking it, little tree?* I waited in silence, conscious that God was impressing something on my spirit. A tree doesn't just stand there and "take it" because it's dormant. It's still alive. It bears the weight of snow because snow is important. Some branches will break off. Weaker than the others, they needed to. As the snow melts, it will eventually water roots that will promote spring's growth, though it seems in the far distant future.

What connection is there between Christmas snow and our celebration of the moment Christ drew His first breath in Bethlehem? The popular Christmas song about Mary could be remade into "Jesus, Did You Know?" Yes. Jesus knew before He was conceived what was being asked of Him. In eternity past, He knew that the tiny hands Mary checked for intact fingers would one day be pierced. That the human experience Jesus stepped into for our sake was temporary and hard. That the weight of what was being asked of Him, both in life and in His death, would be vital for our redemption. Jesus took our transgressions on His shoulders so our scarlet sins could be made white as snow. *Thank You, Jesus.* —CYNTHIA RUCHTI

FAITH STEP: *This Christmas Day, let your heart rest on the wonder that if there were no Nativity—no God in the flesh—there would be no white-as-snow.*

WEDNESDAY, DECEMBER 25

Those who went ahead and those who followed shouted, "Hosanna!"
"Blessed is he who comes in the name of the Lord!" Mark 11:9 (NIV)

WE HAD JUST FINISHED OUR Christmas service and were filing out of the sanctuary. The sermon had been especially inspiring, and it was impossible to deny the Christmas spirit.

My 10-year-old son, Steven, was no different from the rest of the congregation. He had been enthralled by the message and sung the songs with enthusiasm. I wondered what had come over him. As we made our way toward the door, Steven exclaimed, "I love church!" Everyone turned to look at him in awe. I have to admit, a bit of pridefulness entered my heart. Was it the children's Bible we read before bedtime each evening? Or maybe our habit of praying at meals had made him so spiritual. No matter the reason, it was obvious to everyone, I had done something right.

"Why do you love church?" I asked him, my voice a bit louder than usual. I couldn't wait for everyone to hear what a wonderful job I had been doing.

"Because we pray to Santa!" he said with enthusiasm. I felt my face get hot. "Oh, you know we don't pray to Santa," I said.

"Yes, we do!" At the top of his lungs, Steven sang, "Oh Santa, oh Santa, oh Santa in the highest!"

Laughter erupted around me. There was nothing to do except join in. That Christmas night, I opened the children's Bible to the Easter story. I had a lot of explaining to do about the meaning of hosanna. —JEANNIE HUGHES

FAITH STEP: *Think of a time your words were misunderstood and you could laugh about it.*

THE BIRTH OF JESUS

IN THOSE DAYS CAESAR AUGUSTUS issued a decree that a census should be taken of the entire Roman world. (This was the first census that took place while Quirinius was governor of Syria.) And everyone went to their own town to register.

So Joseph also went up from the town of Nazareth in Galilee to Judea, to Bethlehem the town of David, because he belonged to the house and line of David. He went there to register with Mary, who was pledged to be married to him and was expecting a child. While they were there, the time came for the baby to be born, and she gave birth to her firstborn, a son. She wrapped him in cloths and placed him in a manger, because there was no guest room available for them.

And there were shepherds living out in the fields nearby, keeping watch over their flocks at night. An angel of the Lord appeared to them, and the glory of the Lord shone around them, and they were terrified. But the angel said to them, "Do not be afraid. I bring you good news that will cause great joy for all the people. Today in the town of David a Savior has been born to you; he is the Messiah, the Lord. This will be a sign to you: You will find a baby wrapped in cloths and lying in a manger."

Suddenly a great company of the heavenly host appeared with the angel, praising God and saying,

> "Glory to God in the highest heaven,
> and on earth peace to those on whom his favor rests."

When the angels had left them and gone into heaven, the shepherds said to one another, "Let's go to Bethlehem and see this thing that has happened, which the Lord has told us about."

So they hurried off and found Mary and Joseph, and the baby, who was lying in the manger. When they had seen him, they spread the word concerning what had been told them about this child, and all who heard it were amazed at what the shepherds said to them. But Mary treasured up all these things and pondered them in her heart. The shepherds returned, glorifying and praising God for all the things they had heard and seen, which were just as they had been told. —Luke 2:1–20 (NIV)

Advent and Christmas 2024
Reflections and Memories

Advent and Christmas 2024
Reflections and Memories

CONTRIBUTORS

Isabella Campolattaro 6, 20, 36, 56, 76
Pat Butler Dyson 10, 23, 53, 67, 77
Gwen Ford Faulkenberry 30, 41, 45, 61, 73
Heidi Gaul 8, 22, 55, 62, 71, 79
Jeannie Hughes 5, 21, 52, 63, 82
Gloria Joyce 14, 29, 37, 47, 66
Jeanette Levellie 28, 35, 39, 60, 68
Ericka Loynes 16, 31, 43, 51, 65

Erin Keeley Marshall 17, 38, 54, 69, 80
Dianne Neal Matthews 13, 27, 34, 42, 57
Claire McGarry 9, 24, 32, 49, 59
Jennifer Anne F. Messing 11, 19, 50, 75
Cynthia Ruchti 15, 44, 58, 74, 81
Emily E. Ryan 12, 33, 40, 46, 72
Kristen West 7, 18, 25, 64, 78

ACKNOWLEDGMENTS

Every attempt has been made to credit the sources of copyrighted material used in this book. If any such acknowledgment has been inadvertently omitted or miscredited, receipt of such information would be appreciated.

Scripture quotations marked (AMPC) are taken from the *Amplified Bible, Classic Edition*. Copyright © 1954, 1958, 1962, 1964, 1965, 1987 by The Lockman Foundation.

Scripture quotations marked (CEB) are taken from the *Common English Bible*. Copyright © 2011 by Common English Bible.

Scripture quotations marked (CJB) are taken from the *Complete Jewish Bible* by David H. Stern. Copyright © 1998. All rights reserved. Used by permission of Messianic Jewish Publishers, 6120 Day Long Lane, Clarksville, MD 21029. messianicjewish.net.

Scripture quotations marked (ESV) are taken from *The Holy Bible, English Standard Version*. Copyright © 2001 by Crossway Bibles, a division of Good News Publishers. Used by permission. All rights reserved.

Scripture quotations marked (GW) are taken from *GOD'S WORD*°. Copyright © 1995, 2003, 2013, 2014, 2019, 2020 by God's Word to the Nations Mission Society. Used by permission.

Scripture quotations marked (MSG) are taken from *The Message*. Copyright © 1993, 2002, 2018 by Eugene H. Peterson.

Scripture quotations marked (NCV) are taken from *The Holy Bible, New Century Version*. Copyright © 2005 by Thomas Nelson.

Scripture quotations marked (NIV) are taken from *The Holy Bible, New International Version*°, *NIV*°. Copyright © 1973, 1978, 1984, 2011 by Biblica, Inc. Used by permission. All rights reserved worldwide.

Scripture quotations marked (NKJV) are taken from the *New King James Version*°. Copyright © 1982 by Thomas Nelson. Used by permission. All rights reserved.

Scripture quotations marked (NLT) are taken from the *Holy Bible, New Living Translation*. Copyright © 1996, 2004, 2007, 2015 by Tyndale House Foundation. Used by permission of Tyndale House Publishers Inc., Carol Stream, Illinois. All rights reserved.

Scripture quotations marked (NLV) are from the *New Life Version* of the Bible, copyright © 1969, 2003 by Barbour Publishing Inc.

Scripture quotations marked (TLB) are taken from *The Living Bible*. Copyright © 1971 by Tyndale House Publishers, Inc., Carol Stream, Illinois. All rights reserved.

Scripture quotations marked (TPT) are taken from *The Passion Translation*°, copyright © 2017, 2018, 2020 by Passion & Fire Ministries, Inc. Used by permission. All rights reserved.

Thank you to Bob Hostetler for allowing us to use "An Advent Prayer."

A Note from the Editors

We hope you enjoyed *Walking with Jesus: Devotions for Advent & Christmas 2024,* published by Guideposts. For over 75 years, Guideposts, a nonprofit organization, has been driven by a vision of a world filled with hope. We aspire to be the voice of a trusted friend, a friend who makes you feel more hopeful and connected.

By making a purchase from Guideposts, you join our community in touching millions of lives, inspiring them to believe that all things are possible through faith, hope, and prayer. Your continued support allows us to provide uplifting resources to those in need. Whether through our communities, websites, apps, or publications, we inspire our audiences, bring them together, and comfort, uplift, entertain, and guide them. Visit us at guideposts.org to learn more.

We would love to hear from you. Write us at Guideposts, P.O. Box 5815, Harlan, Iowa 51593 or call us at (800) 932-2145. Did you love *Walking with Jesus: Devotions for Advent & Christmas 2024*? Leave a review for this product on guideposts.org/shop. Your feedback helps others in our community find relevant products.

Find inspiration, find faith, find Guideposts.

Shop our best sellers and favorites at
guideposts.org/shop
Or scan the QR code to go directly to our Shop